NAMED TRAINS on L N E R LINES

by

W.B. YEADON

Part II:
Streamlined Trains, Boat Trains, Holiday Trains, Business Trains, Officially Nameless Trains & Developments by British Railways.

The catalogue reference relating to the material used in this album is as follows:
DYE/1/118, DYE/1/119, DYE/1/120.

This second part of Named Trains on LNER lines
is dedicated to a Yorkshire couple by the name of Yeadon from Yeadon.

First published in the United Kingdom by Book Law Publications
382 Carlton Hill, Nottingham, NG4 1JA.
Printed and bound by The Amadeus Press, Cleckheaton, West Yorkshire.

Contents

List of named train featured in this Part viii

The Streamlined Trains 155

The Boat Trains 175

The Business Trains 210

The Holiday Trains 221

Officially Nameless 251

Developments by British Railways 258

Decorations on Headboards 301

BR Period Holiday Trains 303

LNER Pacifics on LMS Scottish Named Trains 308

The named trains featured in Part II

The Boat Trains:
>HOOK CONTINENTAL
>ANTWERP CONTINENTAL
>ESBJERG CONTINENTAL
>SCANDINAVIAN CONTINENTAL
>SCANDINAVIAN
>FLUSHING CONTINENTAL
>THE DAY CONTINENTAL
>NORTH COUNTRY CONTINENTAL
>NORWEGIAN BOAT EXPRESS
>NORSEMAN

The Holiday Trains:
>NORFOLK COAST EXPRESS
>FIFE COAST EXPRESS
>LOTHIAN COAST EXPRESS
>SCARBOROUGH FLIER
>NORTHERN BELLE
>SCOUTS CRUISE
>B.L.A. and B.A.O.R. Leave Trains

The Streamlined Trains:
>THE SILVER JUBILEE
>CORONATION
>WEST RIDING LIMITED

The Business Trains:
>EAST ANGLIAN
>THE MASTER CUTLER

Officially Nameless Trains:
>PORTS TO PORTS EXPRESS
>ABERDEEN - PENZANCE SERVICE
>GARDEN CITIES & CAMBRIDGE BUFFET EXPRESS

DEVELOPMENTS BY BRITISH RAILWAYS

Trains on ex-LNER lines named by British Railways:
>THE SOUTH YORKSHIREMAN
>TEES - TYNE PULLMAN
>THE NORFOLKMAN
>THE CAPITALS LIMITED
>THE ELIZABETHAN
>THE WHITE ROSE
>THE WEST RIDING
>THE FENMAN
>THE NORTHUMBRIAN
>THE NORTH BRITON
>THE TYNESIDER
>THE EASTERLING
>THE BROADSMAN
>THE HEART OF MIDLOTHIAN
>THE TALISMAN
>THE FAIR MAID
>THE ESSEX COAST EXPRESS
>THE TEES - THAMES
>ANGLO - SCOTTISH CAR CARRIER

THE STREAMLINED TRAINS

THE SILVER JUBILEE

CORONATION

WEST RIDING LIMITED

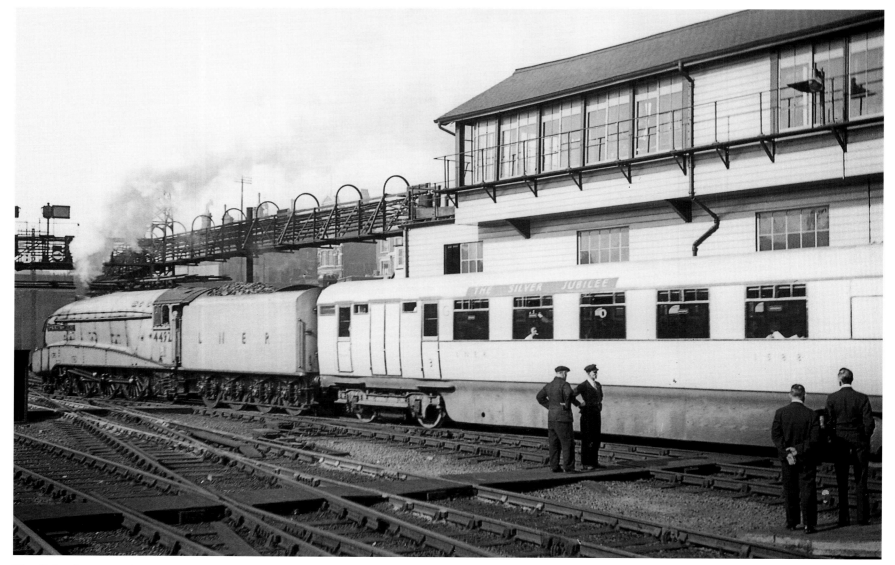

The distinctive streamline skirting of *THE SILVER JUBILEE* set is apparent in this view of a Down service leaving King's Cross in 1938 behind A4 No.4492 DOMINION OF NEW ZEALAND. The 5.30 p.m. departure from London was a favourite with businessmen who were able to relax, take an aperitif and have dinner during the four hour dash to Newcastle.

THE SILVER JUBILEE

The A4 Class engines which were built from September 1935 immediately put the LNER into a different league on express haulage by steam. Their achievements were never beaten or even narrowly approached. Gresley was sufficiently confident that development of his basic Pacific design would enable these engines to maintain a regular year-round weekday service linking Newcastle and London in four hours.

Introduced as *THE SILVER JUBILEE* on Monday 30th September 1935, the train then ran Mondays to Fridays, doing return trips until Friday 1st September 1939. By the following Monday we were at war, and running high-speed trains was no longer feasible. That was then the end for this particular named train.

With much of its journey having to be run at over 90 m.p.h., a headboard, secured only by a spring clip was an unacceptable risk, so one was never carried. Careful thought in the design of engine and coaches had eliminated all possible excrescence, so even roof boards on the coaches were not used. Instead, the train name was painted in their style on each coach. The engine's wedge shaped front end was so novel and outstanding that recognition of it was immediate and for some two years *THE SILVER JUBILEE* had the field to itself. Out on the line its speed was such that it would approach an observer too quickly for reading its name easily, but this could be done as the train receded into the distance. The removable cover for the corridor vestibule connection on the rear of the last carriage thus carried the train name prominently displayed in black letters on the silver-grey background.

Throughout its almost four years life, its schedule was unchanged. Ex Newcastle at 10.00 a.m., it just made a call at Darlington and was into King's Cross at 2.00 p.m. Whilst in London the Rexine covered coach bodies were washed and their interior given a full servicing. Then it left at 5.30 p.m., made the Darlington call, and arrived in Newcastle at 9.30 p.m.

Except for the very rare occasions of rostered engine failure, it was a King's Cross shed A4 class working, and although less than three weeks old, the first of the class, No.2509 SILVER LINK, did all ten round trips in the first two weeks. Then until into 1937, Nos.2510 QUICKSILVER and 2512 SILVER FOX shared the duty, and it was most unusual for the reserve engine at Gateshead shed, No.2511 SILVER KING, to be seen on the train. From 1937, blue became standard colour for the streamlined trains, and during 1938 the set of silver-grey coaches were repainted to suit, with train name still painted at cant rail level. From 1938 there was a spare set of coaches available to serve the three high-speed services and that set did not have any train indication, so that when used for *THE SILVER JUBILEE*, that train ran anonymously.

Post-war *THE SILVER JUBILEE* did not resume as such, and the set of coaches, which had been in storage, was put to other use. The triple articulated dining set continued to work between Newcastle and London in the *NORTHUMBRIAN*, but the other five coaches moved to Scottish Region of BR and worked in the *FIFE COAST EXPRESS*.

(right) The rear of *THE SILVER JUBILEE* as the train comes off the King Edward bridge at Newcastle at the start of its journey to London. For nearly two years this was the only streamlined train on the LNER and was extremely popular with businessmen. Its initial make-up of seven coaches, as seen here, was soon increased to eight to accommodate its regular clientele.

A4 No.4493 WOODCOCK was new in July 1937 and its livery was green from that date to July of the following year when it was repainted into Garter blue. So, this picture of it hauling a Down service of *THE SILVER JUBILEE* at Darlington must date from that period, more than likely the summer of 1937. At this time the engine was based at Gateshead and here was probably standing in for the rostered engine which had failed.

Except for a short period of 3¹/₂ months based at Gateshead shed, A4 No.4485 KESTREL spent the first two years of its life working from Haymarket shed, much of that time in green livery and therefore not totally eligible to work the streamline trains. However, a change to Garter blue paint in December 1937 and then a transfer to King's Cross shed in March 1939 brought it further into the reckoning for hauling either of the three streamlined trains as here in 1939 at Croft with *THE SILVER JUBILEE*. Of all the A4's only one was never employed on a streamlined train - the last of the class No.4903 PEREGRINE. Based at Doncaster shed throughout the remaining period of the Streamline Era, and employed mostly on the *YORKSHIRE PULLMAN* working, that is not too surprising.

Three instances of non-A4 haulage of *THE SILVER JUBILEE*: *(above)* Gateshead based A3 No.2501 COLOMBO works through Peterborough with the Up train at an unknown date. *(inset, opposite)* C1 No.4446 looks completely out of place in this winter scene on the 28th December 1938. The C1 had taken over from ailing A4 No.2510 at Peterborough. *(opposite)* Heading towards London in June 1938, these two engines, D2 No.4379 and C1 No.3293, are all that New England shed could muster for the final leg from Peterborough.

With its chime whistle sounding a greeting, A4 No.2512 speeds northward with the Down *CORONATION* near Ranskill during the summer of 1938. Already this London - Edinburgh service had been running for a year and during that time the tenders of the A4's were modified to enable a greater coal load to be carried. This decision was made after numerous instances during the previous winter when the engines reached their destination with barely enough, or as in a few cases, no coal in the tender.

CORONATION

The success of the first high-speed train led to consideration of running a similar one between London and Edinburgh on a six-hour timing. Even through the 1935-1936 winter, it had proved that the 4-hour schedule on the Newcastle train could be maintained regularly. So proof was needed that the run on to Edinburgh could be done in no more than two hours. Trial was made on 26th September 1936, which was a Saturday, so that *THE SILVER JUBILEE* stock could be used, and to it was added the dynamometer car. The reserve engine, No.2511 SILVER KING, reached Edinburgh three minutes inside the two hours for the 124^1/$_2$ miles, so the project was feasible.

On *THE SILVER JUBILEE*, one set of coaches could make the return trip each day, at times convenient and acceptable to business passengers but the new service to Edinburgh would require two sets. The Down train left King's Cross at 4.00 p.m., had a three minute call at York, and reached Edinburgh at 10.00 p.m. The Up train left Waverley at 4.30 p.m., called only at Newcastle, and was into London at 10.30 p.m. These calls allowed crews to be changed, but the engines worked the full 392.6 miles. Both trains were always rostered for haulage by A4 class engines shedded at King's Cross and Haymarket, and they were usually those which had a corridor tender, but others did take this working, Nos.4466 HERRING GULL, 4467 WILD SWAN and 4902 SEAGULL all being used by King's Cross shed.

On Monday 5th July 1937 this London-Edinburgh high-speed service began, and with Royal permission, the two trains carried the name *CORONATION*. No headboard was carried, but each coach was embellished with the name centrally placed in 6in. high stainless steel Gill sans letters. Their slight addition to wind resistance was accepted for their attractive look.

When these trains ran mainly in daylight, an observation saloon was attached to the rear and on the end it also showed *CORONATION* across the full width. When this beaver tail shaped coach was not included, the cover of the corridor connection of the last coach carried the name in white lettering on the blue background.

This prestigious and popular train was fated to have a life of only two years and two months. Its final runs being on Friday 1st September 1939, and the war then caused its demise. The two sets of coaches were put into storage, and after the conflict, the *CORONATION* names were removed, and some modifications were made to them. They were then split up and put to a variety of other uses, including Edinburgh-Aberdeen, King's Cross-Glasgow, Manchester-Cleethorpes and London (Liverpool Street)-Yarmouth. The only named train to get any was *THE WEST RIDING* on the London-Leeds service. It was in this train that one of the twin Firsts was destroyed by fire near Huntingdon on 14th July 1951. The two beaver tail units continued to be used as observation saloons, one going on to the West Highland line working through to Mallaig during the summer seasons.

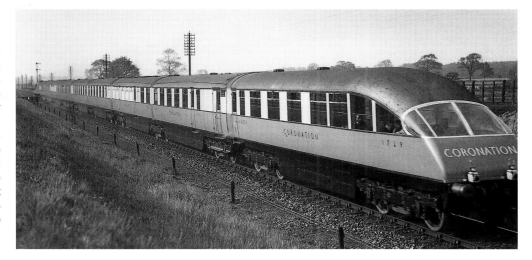

The rear of the same Down train seen in the previous view near Ranskill. The stainless steel letters making up the name of the train can be easily discerned from this angle. The beaver-tail coach making up the ninth vehicle of the set was only attached during the period of the Summer timetable so that during the winter months the *CORONATION* became an eight-coach formation.

The rear of one of the winter service trains showing the adorned vestibule connection cover. All three LNER streamlined services had this rear end style of identification during the winter period and the Newcastle and Leeds services carried them all year round.

The Up CORONATION speedily recedes towards London as seen from the observation car on the Down train. This fleeting meet took place daily around Wiske Moor water troughs and no doubt added to the enjoyment of the journey.

At the start of its long but rapid journey north, the *CORONATION* exits Gasworks Tunnel behind A4 No.4467 WILD SWAN in 1938.

To be ready for the inaugural run of the *CORONATION*, five new A4's, Nos.4488-4492 were given the names of Commonwealth countries. No.4491, new in June 1937, was named COMMONWEALTH OF AUSTRALIA and here is on an Up service climbing Cockburnspath bank during those first weeks of service. This particular A4 had worked the first Down service to Edinburgh where it was shedded and, during the next ten weeks the engine hauled no less than forty-eight of the services run.

Both the Up and Down services of the *CORONATION* spent most of the winter months travelling through darkness and therefore photographs of the train in a winter setting are virtually unknown. However, the Up train's station stop at Newcastle enabled photographers to get the occasional shot although conditions were far from perfect. This is 4467 WILD SWAN at Newcastle (Central) on Wednesday 11th January 1939 making the early evening stop for a crew change.

Although the A4's had a superb reputation for reliability, they were not immune from the occasional quirk. Here on 9th March 1938, York based V2 No.4782, hauling the Down *CORONATION*, deputises for a failed A4 at Darlington.

Another instance of night photography being necessary was to capture the arrival of the Up train at King's Cross. No.4492 still appears immaculate after its near 400-mile run in 1938. This engine was one of those which was affected by shortage of coal capacity in the first winter of the service; forced to stop at Hitchin with the Up train on Thursday night 9th December 1937, and being assisted to London by C1 No.4427.

(below) At some time in the summer of 1938, A3 No.2744 GRAND PARADE had to deputise for a failed A4. The engine was Doncaster based at this period but from where it took over this Down train seen at Darlington, is unknown. On another occasion in 1938, Gateshead A1 No.2575 GALOPIN stepped in for an A4.

The inaugural *WEST RIDING LIMITED* ready to depart from Leeds (Central) on Monday 27th September 1937 for its non-stop run to London. A4 No.4495 had entered traffic in late August painted green and carrying the name GREAT SNIPE but in order to give the engine a more appropriate name, and livery, for its intended employment on the Leeds-London non-stop, it returned to works on 12th September and emerged painted Garter blue and with its new name GOLDEN FLEECE which it carried to withdrawal. The next A4 out, No.4496, was also suitably named with a connection to the woollen industry - GOLDEN SHUTTLE. It was available to take its turn hauling the *WEST RIDING LIMITED* during the first week of the new service.

WEST RIDING LIMITED

From early Great Northern Railway days there had always been lucrative traffic emanating from Bradford and Leeds to and from King's Cross. This was augmented by the buyers of Australian and New Zealand wool who needed to attend the auctions held in London. Having established successful high-speed services for Newcastle and Edinburgh, Leeds and Bradford needed to be treated similarly. So when the special stock for the *CORONATION* was ordered, a third set (but no beaver tail) was included, which enabled a Monday to Friday high-speed service for the two Yorkshire cities to start on Monday 27th September 1937.

Named *WEST RIDING LIMITED,* the train left Bradford (Exchange) hauled by a pair of Class N2 0-6-2T's at 11.10 a.m. and after reversal at Leeds, departed at 11.31 a.m. for King's Cross behind an A4. A connecting train from Halifax at 10.40 a.m. enabled passengers to join the train at Bradford, and for their return they left Leeds at 10.14 p.m. to arrive 10.51 p.m. at Halifax (Old) station.

The named train was non-stop between Leeds and London, and its descriptive brochure clearly indicated that it was only intended for passengers to and from London, hence the inclusion of the word 'Limited' in the title. Like the other two high-speed trains, it made its last run on Friday 1st September 1939, the war then causing its cancellation. The eight coaches were then stored in the carriage shed at Copley Hill, Leeds and, during the war, emerged occasionally for the axles to be turned and to avoid flats developing on the wheels.

Post-war, the *WEST RIDING LIMITED* was not restored as such, but from 23rd May 1949, a new service between Leeds and London began named *THE WEST RIDING,* and its stock included six refurbished coaches from its streamlined predecessor. These had been repainted to the British Railways new standard of crimson and cream.

For the short stretch between Bradford (Exchange) and Leeds (Central) and because a reversal was necessary at the latter place, two N2's were employed between those points, however, slick running was the daily order because only twenty-one minutes were allowed between the Bradford and Leeds departures. Nos.2688 and 2584 were both Copley Hill engines.

Headboards were deemed unnecessary and even dangerous for the streamlined trains and the *WEST RIDING LIMITED* was no exception, its two and three-quarter hour dash to King's Cross included a lot of high speed running once the East Coast Main Line was gained. Here No.4495 gets the first train underway.

No.4496 takes its turn with the eight-coach *WEST RIDING LIMITED* and is seen on the ECML with the Up service in 1938. The service had run for less than two years when war brought its demise.

(below) When war signalled the end of the Yorkshire to London streamlined service in September 1939, the stock was stored inside the carriage shed at Copley Hill and occasionally it was shunted around the precincts of the shed in order that the wheel bearings did not seize. Copley Hill J50 No.599 was itself less than a year old at the outbreak of hostilities in 1939 but unlike the eight streamlined coaches it is moving here, it would remain active throughout the war.

After nearly three years of employment on streamline haulage, A4 No.2510 passes Low Fell in the early evening during July 1938 with the Up *CORONATION*. The reliability of these outstanding engines enabled the LNER to maintain an enviable record of punctuality for their three streamline services. This particular train would have stopped for a crew change at Newcastle (Central) but the locomotive itself would stay with the train for the duration of the journey. Just over one year later, this immaculate scene would become simply a memory.

THE BOAT TRAINS

HOOK CONTINENTAL
ANTWERP CONTINENTAL
ESBJERG CONTINENTAL
SCANDINAVIAN CONTINENTAL
SCANDINAVIAN
FLUSHING CONTINENTAL
THE DAY CONTINENTAL
NORTH COUNTRY CONTINENTAL
NORWEGIAN BOAT EXPRESS
NORSEMAN

B12 No.8558 and the new eleven-coach 'Continental Express' set pose on Brentwood bank for this publicity photograph at some time in 1925. The B12 was a Stratford engine at this time whereas the service trains were normally hauled by Parkeston based B12's. Notice the roof boards on the passenger coaches only.

HOOK CONTINENTAL

At the start of the LNER, the steamer services from Harwich were to and from Holland, Belgium and Denmark, each normally provided with a boat train from and to London (Liverpool Street). The 1923/ 1924 timetables simply described them as 'Continental Restaurant & Pullman Car Expresses'. The Pullman component stemmed from the agreement which the Great Eastern Railway had made with the Pullman Car Company Ltd. in 1920 and which, after a reluctant start, the LNER then developed very successfully and extensively.

In the 1923 timetable the train for Hook of Holland passengers left Liverpool Street at 8.30 p.m. to arrive 10.15 p.m. at Parkeston Quay, where the Up train left at 7.02 a.m. for a London arrival at 8.38 a.m. For this service the LNER built a new eleven-coach set like the two 'Flying Scotsman' sets of September 1924; this third set was put to work between London and Parkeston Quay. On Monday 30th March 1925 that train was named *HOOK CONTINENTAL*, although the title was only carried by the coach roof boards. Limited to passengers for the Hook of Holland - or further - it normally departed from Liverpool Street station at 8.30 p.m. and in addition to the LNER coaches, it included two first class Pullman cars. The train returned the following morning, due into Liverpool Street at around 8 o'clock - when the boat had arrived at its scheduled time. Alternative paths were shown in the working timetable for use if the boat was delayed by adverse weather or otherwise, as often happened in the winter months.

Although some of the 1925 coaches were extensively refurbished in 1936, a complete new train of ten coaches was built and began work in 1938.

That new train had luxurious interiors akin to those of the *CORONATION* streamlined train of the previous year, in both the 1st and 2nd class coaches. The war inevitably caused cancellation of all the continental services, and the 2nd class coaches were redeployed as thirds from July 1942. The 1939-45 conflict also saw the end of Pullman car inclusion in the *HOOK CONTINENTAL* because they were not restored when that service was resumed on Wednesday 14th November 1945, to run three times a week at first, but then reverting to daily running (except on Sundays) from 30th September 1946.

Until January 1929 motive power was provided by B12/1 class engines shedded at Parkeston, but generally was then taken over by the new Gresley B17 engines, although the former continued to be used after they started to be rebuilt from May 1932 to B12/3. These two classes then regularly did the job until the train ceased to run at the beginning of September 1939. Post-war, the Thompson B1 class superseded them, but normal use of LNER designed engines ceased in the summer of 1951, when the upgrading of the former Great Eastern main lines had been completed. Services were able to be accelerated because the line could then take the new British Railways standard engines of the 4-6-2 'Britannia' class, and they took over all the main duties.

Pre-war, engines hauling the *HOOK CONTINENTAL* surprisingly did not carry a headboard; at least no visible evidence of so doing has surfaced. Even for the publicised first run with the 1938 new stock, engine 8517 of class B12/3 did not have one. This is all the more curious as after the war, a board of pre-war style with square top corners, carrying *HOOK CONTINENTAL* in two lines of black letters on a white background was seen briefly at the Parkeston end. From at least 5th April 1947 a distinctly odd board was in use, B1 No.1008 on the Down train passing Bethnal Green carrying it, as did B1 No.1149 on Thursday 17th July 1947, waiting at Parkeston Quay for boat passengers to disembark. That board, of the same style, simply showed HOOK-OF-HOLLAND also in black on a white background.

During 1950, whilst B1 class engines were still being used, the pre-war type headboard was replaced by a cast plate, which had beaded edges, raised letters, and indented top corners. The name was in three lines (instead of two) as it was now *THE HOOK CONTINENTAL*. The British and Dutch flags were painted on, although later, each flag was on a circular plaque.

An unidentified B12 at Parkeston Quay with the *HOOK CONTINENTAL*.

The first run of the new 1938 stock with B12/3 No.8517 of Stratford in charge and ready to depart Parkeston Quay for London. The carrying of a headboard for this train would not become general practise until after WW2.

The one-line *HOOK-OF-HOLLAND* headboard adorning the front of B1 No.1149 on the Up train at Parkeston Quay in July 1947.

(opposite) The first cast BR headboard showing the three-line full title bestowed on the train from 1950, complete with British and Dutch flags. This is the 6.45 a.m. ex Parkeston Quay arriving at Liverpool Street on the 22nd July 1950.

Thompson's B1 generally took over the working of this train on its post-war resumption. Here one of Parkeston's B1's No.1135 is seen in the summer of 1947 carrying the two-line *HOOK CONTINENTAL* headboard on the 7.15 a.m. ex Parkeston Quay at Shenfield.

ANTWERP CONTINENTAL

This train was always overshadowed by the importance accorded to that for the Hook, which it followed by ten, sometimes fifteen, minutes out of Liverpool Street. It was not restricted to passengers joining the boat either, because after its call at Parkeston Quay, it continued to Harwich Town station, but it catered for those going on the boat to Zeebrugge. In the timetable for 1923 it left Liverpool Street at 8.40 p.m. with a 10.20 p.m. arrival at Parkeston Quay. Subject to the boat's arrival, the Up train left at 6.20 a.m. with a London arrival at 8.00 a.m. Both the Hook and Antwerp boat trains included Pullman cars in their normal make-up.

Apparently regarded as expendable, during the depression of trade years of 1931 and 1932, when there were only enough passengers to justify running one boat train, this was the one which was cancelled, and passengers for Antwerp went along with those for Holland. In the Up direction, both shared the train due out of Parkeston Quay at 6.55 a.m. to reach London at 8.38 a.m. Certainly the Antwerp boat train carried its own coach roof boards, but when headboards were introduced in 1932, their provision did not extend to this particular train. Following the 1931/32 cancellation, there was recovery and by summer 1939, not only was it running again in its own right but it included a Pullman 1st class parlour

car and three of their restaurant cars which with the eight LNER bogie coaches made a load of about 390 tons.

The service to Antwerp was withdrawn at the outbreak of war, and when resumed on Monday 29th July 1946, it only ran on two days each week. Outward passengers had to leave Liverpool Street in coaches attached to the 3.00 p.m. Yarmouth train, from which they were detached at Manningtree to be worked forward locally to Parkeston Quay. Those arriving in this country shared the *HOOK CONTINENTAL* train leaving Parkeston at 7.15 a.m. and due into Liverpool Street at 9.00 a.m. Travel by boat to Antwerp during the post-war years was diminishing and by the time the 1954 timetable was published there was nothing shown for it.

The *ANTWERP CONTINENTAL* boat train was never destined to be memorable. Withdrawn during the Depression years, never having a headboard, running only twice a week in the post-war period and then total oblivion from 1954. However, during its pre-war 'recovery' period it could at one time boast twelve bogie coaches in its make-up including a Pullman 1st parlour and three Pullman restaurant cars. Chadwell Heath.

(opposite) Headboards for the *FLUSHING CONTINENTAL* were displayed for the first time in 1932 by which time B12's had generally given up haulage of the train in favour of B17's. No.8508 was a Parkeston engine when this mid-1930's view was captured at Brentwood.

FLUSHING CONTINENTAL

The steamers operating out of Harwich were owned by the LNER, but those from and to Flushing belonged to the Dutch owned Zeeland Steamship Company. Until the end of 1926, their English port had been Folkestone but from 1st January 1927 they transferred to Harwich Parkeston Quay. The LNER put on appropriately timed trains to serve them and the coaches carried roof boards reading *THE FLUSHING CONTINENTAL*.

From 1932, the engine carried a headboard of the usual type showing just *FLUSHING CONTINENTAL* in two lines. In that year, the Down train left London at 9.30 a.m. and the Up train (which included Pullman restaurant cars) was due out of Parkeston Quay at 6.55 p.m. to reach London at 8.38. In summer 1939, the departure from London was at 10.00 a.m. and return arrival was 9.30 p.m.

During the period 1927 to 1929, B12/1 class had this duty then the train was mainly taken over by B17 class. War caused cessation and when resumed, the train name had to be changed because the boats then used the Hook instead of Flushing. So from 14th June 1947 it became *THE DAY CONTINENTAL* which is described later.

This September 1932 photograph of the *FLUSHING CONTINENTAL* shows B17 No.2824, also of Parkeston shed, in charge of the Down train on Brentwood bank. Note the twin discs indicating boat train, these being later supplemented with a centre lamp.

With five LNER vehicles and three Pullman cars in the train, B17 No.2822 brings the *FLUSHING CONTINENTAL* through the junction at Manningtree circa 1935. This engine spent the majority of its pre-war life working boat trains from either Parkeston or Stratford sheds.

The mainstay of the G.E. main line express motive power, the B12 had charge of most of the boat trains until the advent of the B17. Here, climbing Brentwood bank in the late afternoon of a 1920's summer, No.8533 displays the discs and lamp to signify the status of its train which in this case was the *ESBJERG CONTINENTAL EXPRESS* which later became known as the *SCANDINAVIAN*.

SCANDINAVIAN

Another steamer service using Harwich, linked it with the Danish port of Esbjerg, from where there were express trains to Copenhagen. In the 1923 winter timetable, a Down boat train ran on Mondays, Wednesdays, Thursdays and Saturdays at 3.20 p.m. to reach Parkeston Quay at 5.36 p.m. The corresponding Up train left at 5.30 p.m. to reach London (Liverpool Street) at 7.30 p.m., on Mondays, Tuesdays, Wednesdays and Saturdays. In the summer months, the traffic warranted the LNER running a separate train for it, but outside that period, coaches were attached to a train for Yarmouth and dropped off at Manningtree, to be worked the remaining nine miles to Parkeston Quay. In the summer timetable period, a train with Pullman restaurant cars left Liverpool Street at 4.10 p.m. to run non-stop to Parkeston Quay and then on to Harwich Town station.

The return service was not specifically timed as it depended on the boat's arrival, which was due at 4.45 p.m. The LNER timetables merely showed Liverpool Street arrival would be "About 2½ hours after arrival of vessel at Harwich". Outside the summer period, the coaches for the boat passengers left London with the 3.10 p.m. buffet car express to Yarmouth.

The LNER timetable starting 24th September 1928 listed an *ESBJERG CONTINENTAL EXPRESS* and in the timetable starting Monday 22nd September 1930, this had changed to *SCANDINAVIAN CONTINENTAL EXPRESS*, and from 1st May 1931 it was shown simply as *THE SCANDINAVIAN*.

Pre-war, the separate train was usually hauled by B12 or B17 class engines, and from 1932, carried a curved headboard simply showing *SCANDINAVIAN* in black on a white background.

When *THE SCANDINAVIAN* resumed operation from Monday 3rd June 1945 the name was on a unique shape of plate with curved top but a level base; still with a white background and black letters. They were now in two lines, the upper word curved, but the other one parallel with the base. By August 1950, the shape and style was the same, but it now had lettering in white on a black background. For the 1951 summer, this odd shape had been discarded and a cast plate with beaded edge, raised letters and indented top corners, had replaced it and both words were now curved. Post-war haulage was usually done by B1 class although on 2nd October 1948, B12/3 No.61540 took the down train and 61572 did the same

as late as 26th April 1959. But there must have been something unusual on Thursday 3rd September 1959 because the Up train arrived in Liverpool Street behind an Immingham shedded K3 No.61912, quite a stranger to the G.E. line.

(below) The first type of headboard used for the *SCANDINAVIAN* adorns the front of Parkeston's B17 No.2836, being made ready at Stratford shed for the afternoon job back to Harwich.

(left) Another Parkeston B17, No.2823, has a somewhat easy task near Shenfield with this four vehicle make-up of the *SCANDINAVIAN* during the pre-war period in April 1938.

(below) The strange, though not unique, shaped headboard used immediately after boat train services were resumed following cessation of hostilities in 1945. This particular example, now displaying *THE SCANDINAVIAN*, with black letters on a white background was in use until at least 1950. B12 No.61540 has the Down train in October 1948 at Chelmsford.

This Stratford B17, though carrying the headboard, is not showing the more usual two discs and centre lamp code associated with a boat train. This is the 2.0 p.m. ex Parkeston Quay at Chelmsford on the 10th September 1949.

(right) B17 No.61612 is heading the 2.0 p.m. *SCANDINAVIAN,* at Parkeston Quay on the 2nd July 1950, whilst its smokebox is adorned with yet another example of headboard - this being curved on both upper and lower edges.

(below) B1 No.61264 spent the majority of its working life at Parkeston shed and no doubt hauled many boat trains during that time. Here, leaving Parkeston Quay on 16th August 1950, on its way to London, it has charge of *THE SCANDINAVIAN* during the short period (1950-51) when the headboard had white letters on a black background whilst retaining its nearly unique shape.

(right) Although Thompson B1's handled most workings of this train in the post-war period, Stratford B17's could be regularly seen in charge. No.61606, looking splendid at the head of the Down train in March 1950, is wearing the BR style cast headboard with indented top corners, raised letters and beading around the edges. Note also the British and Danish flags. There is no doubt as to this particular train's status.

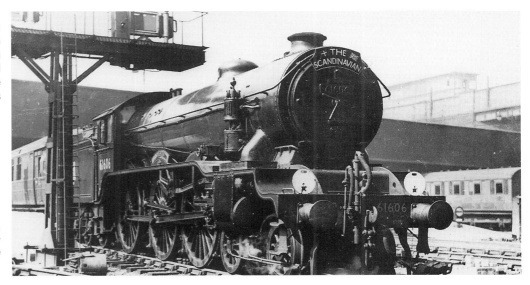

(below) The final style of headboard for this train is carried by 61226, a Parkeston based B1, seen here passing Colchester in the mid-1950's. The only difference from the previous board shows that the two national flags are each sitting on a white background.

Another one of those flat based boards was employed for *THE DAY CONTINENTAL* during early BR days if not before. This is the 9.15 a.m. ex Liverpool Street passing Chelmsford on the 6th August 1949.

Stratford B1 No.61236, a regular within these pages, wearing a more normally shaped board this time, albeit with black letters on a white background. Witham, 16th April 1949.

(opposite) By mid-1950 this cast head board with raised letters, beaded edges, three line legend and national flags, was in general use. Note that 61175, seen here near Chelmsford, is not wearing discs.

THE DAY CONTINENTAL

The service to Holland by the Dutch owned Zeeland Steamship Co. was restored on 14th June 1947 but had moved to Hook of Holland instead of Flushing. The name for the boat train thus changed to *THE DAY CONTINENTAL*, which ran from Liverpool St. at 9.20 a.m. on Tuesdays, Thursdays and Saturdays. From Holland, the boat left about 11.30 a.m. Dutch time on Sundays, Wednesdays and Fridays and in the summer the train was due away from Parkeston Quay at 7.30 p.m. with arrival at 9.15 p.m. in London (Liverpool Street). From Saturday 1st November the train left at 6.35 p.m. for an 8.07 p.m. arrival. By 1950 the service was running on a daily basis, including Saturdays, at around the same timings.

These boat trains included a restaurant car and were worked by engines from Stratford shed. Normally a Class B1 was used but occasionally, as on 5th November 1950, Class B12/3 No.61568 took out the train from Liverpool Street. Curiously class B17 engines were rarely seen on this particular boat train; but there were odd appearances by BR 'Britannia' class 4-6-2's in the 1950's.

When the train became *THE DAY CONTINENTAL*, a curved nameplate with black letters on a white background was employed. This was followed by another of those boards which had a curved top but a flat base. This gave way, in early BR days, to a curved headboard with indented corners which had a white background with the name displayed in two lines of black letters. By mid-1950, this had been superseded by a cast plate of the same shape but with the name in three lines displaying the British and Dutch flags.

Stratford shed would send out their newest suitable motive power on this train.

(opposite) 61236 again, but this time displaying the last example of BR-style headboard with the white background for the national flags. Liverpool Street.

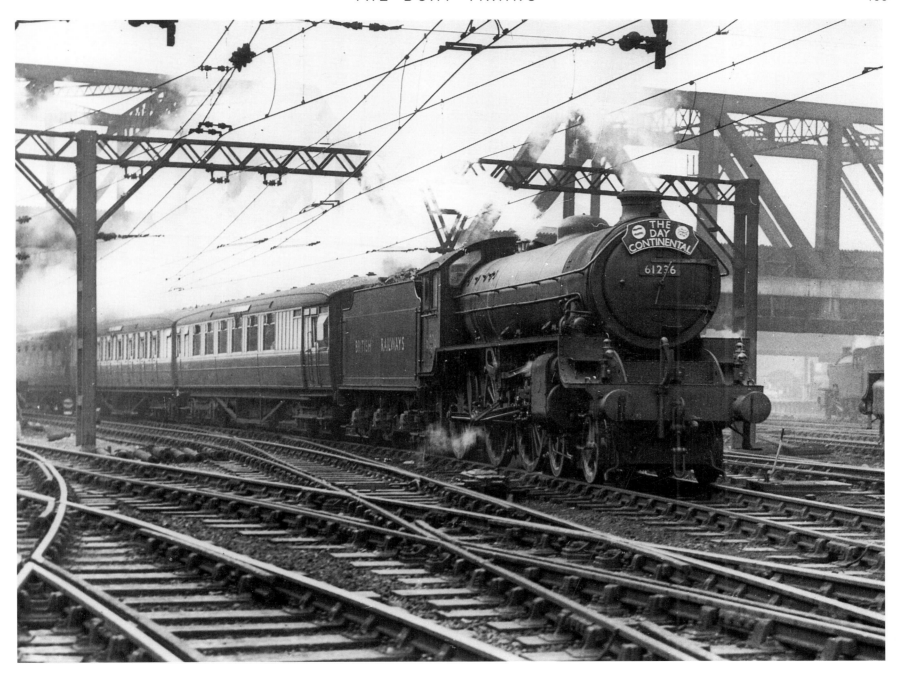

B1's remained the mainstay motive power for this train throughout the 1950's. This is Stratford's No.61280 at Parkeston Quay on the 14th May 1956.

(opposite) As mentioned previously, Stratford usually put their better motive power on this train but BR Britannia No.70037 was a representative of their best. With the engine and the headboard suitably polished and burnished, they appear made-to-measure for each other.

Gorton based B12 No.8557 heads down the Longdendale valley with the Manchester and Liverpool portion of the *NORTH COUNTRY CONTINENTAL* in 1927. This engine would have worked to Ipswich with the Up train on the previous day, the crew lodging overnight in East Anglia. The B12 was based at Gorton for a year from 18th April 1927, having the same crew throughout that period. At the end of March 1928, No.8557 was relieved of its duty and sent to Parkeston. Meanwhile another B12, No.8538 from Ipswich shed then took over the Gorton 'Continental' job until the following February when B17's generally took on that work.

NORTH COUNTRY CONTINENTAL

Although very widely known as such, this train never had any official title and the roof boards on the coaches showed the names of the places which it served. Its origin was as far back as 1885 and was due to the considerable trade that Manchester was doing with the Continent through the port of Harwich. In 1891 the first G.E.R. restaurant car was included in it, and that vehicle led the country by allowing third class passengers to use it. When the train changed to LNER ownership, it started from (and returned to) Liverpool (Central) and Birmingham (New Street). Probably it was inclusion of the latter, which deterred any chance of it being named officially; because no way could Birmingham have accepted association with any 'North Country' title. So in the timetables it never rated higher distinction than 'Continental Restaurant Car Express'.

The portion from Liverpool left Central station at 2.30 p.m., Manchester (Central) at 3.25, Sheffield (Victoria) at 4.42, Workshop at 5.06, Lincoln at 5.56 and Spalding at 6.44 to arrive March at 7.08 p.m. There it collected the portion which had left Birmingham (New St) at 4.00 p.m., Coventry at 4.30, Rugby 5.05 and Peterborough (East) at 6.42 to arrive March at 7.02 p.m. The combined train then left at 7.16 p.m. via Ely, Bury St Edmunds and Ipswich for a 9.38 p.m. arrival at Parkeston Quay. Incoming passengers left Parkeston Quay at 8.02 a.m. and the two portions terminated thus: Liverpool (Central) at 3.20 p.m. and Birmingham (New Street) at 3.15 p.m., the Liverpool portion retaining the restaurant cars.

Beginning 14th May 1927 the working arrangement was changed considerably as engine and crew then went through between Ipswich and Manchester (216 miles) which they worked in reverse on the following day. This eliminated engine changing at March, Lincoln and Sheffield and led to engines from Ipswich being transferred to Gorton shed. These were B12/1 class until the new B17 class engines became available in 1929, and subsequently it was most unusual to see anything other than that class on the Ipswich-Manchester section. This change also gave a much better service to York, a through portion joining and being detached from the main train at Lincoln.

Taking February 1932 as an example, and assuming scheduled arrival of the steamer, the *NORTH COUNTRY CONTINENTAL* left Parkeston Quay at 7.25 a.m. Should the steamer be late, that train was not held awaiting it and "passengers holding tickets for the Midlands and North may travel via London". So this train reached March at 9.56 a.m. and detached the Birmingham portion which was due in New Street station at 1.16 p.m. The main train arrived in Lincoln at 11.22 a.m. from where the York coaches departed at 11.35 a.m. to terminate in York at 1.27 p.m. The Manchester and Liverpool portion - with the restaurant cars - had left Lincoln at 11.30 a.m. and then called at Workshop, Sheffield, Guide Bridge, Manchester (Central), Warrington (Central) to arrive in Liverpool (Central) at 3.00 p.m.

To catch the night boat from Harwich, the three portions respectively left Liverpool at 2.05 p.m., York at 3.25 p.m. and Birmingham at 3.55 p.m., for the complete train to arrive at 9.16 p.m. in Parkeston Quay station. In that direction there was also a through coach included in the York section which had left Glasgow (Queen Street) at 8.37 a.m. but those going north of York had to change there into the *FLYING SCOTSMAN*.

When this train ceased to run on the outbreak of the war on 3rd September 1939, arrival times were 1.04 p.m. at Birmingham, 1.12 p.m. at York and 2.43 p.m. at Liverpool. Departure of the three portions was Liverpool at 2.20 p.m., York (with the Glasgow coach which had left at 8.55 a.m.) at 3.30 p.m., and at 4.00 p.m. from Birmingham.

Although the steamer service was quite quickly resumed after the war, the final LNER timetable included no mention of any Continental Restaurant Car Express to Liverpool, York and Birmingham. In 1949 a buffet car train was put on from Harwich but only to Sheffield, this later being extended to Liverpool (Central) via Manchester (Central). In later BR days, before the closure of the Woodhead route but as steam traction in general was being withdrawn, the service terminated in Manchester.

After 1927 when B12 and B17 engines did all the work - including the Harwich-Ipswich leg, and then through to Manchester, there was still some locomotive interest to be seen on the sections furthest away from the port. Beyond Peterborough East the LMS hauled the portion through to Birmingham. A Lincoln engine (usually D9 class 5113) took on the coaches from there to York, and returned with the Up train but this changed from 1927 to a York turn and for two years they used one of their D20 class. On 2nd February 1929, that was No.1665 which merited comment as one rarely seen at Lincoln. Before the end of that year new D49 class engines had taken over, Nos.253, 336 and then 247 being seen most frequently.

B17 No.2806 has charge of the train in 1929. Still with its number on the tender, this B17 has another ten years of employment on this train before war brought about the abolition of steamer services.

With the engine from Ipswich ending its long run at the buffer stops in Manchester (Central), another engine took care of the run to and from Liverpool. Until into the 1930's four D6 class normally monopolised this duty, 5857 and 5876 from Trafford Park, with 5859 and 5869 of Liverpool Brunswick sheds. They were superseded in the early 1930's when more intensive diagramming brought Sheffield based C1 Atlantics to work the 'Continental' between Manchester and Liverpool. A further change at the end of November 1936 saw a Gorton shedded K3 rostered for this duty and one of them, No.3817, was very lucky not to be derailed on 4th October 1937 when speed was misjudged on the sharply curved entry to Liverpool Central's No.1 Platform and it fouled the coping stones of the platform edge.

The eventual resumption saw the Ipswich engine coming off the train at Sheffield (Victoria) where, from 1954, electric traction took over as far as Guide Bridge. At the latter place steam locomotives took over again for the short trip to Manchester (Central), by this time anything from a Thompson L1 to an ex-LMS 2-6-4T, or a B1 to a 'Jubilee' could be seen powering the rake of Gresley coaches. After reversal in Central the short haul to Liverpool could produce virtually anything at the head end. Once diesel traction had taken over the majority of the GE Line expresses, BR 'Britannia' Pacifics became regular visitors to Sheffield but they too gave way to Stratford based English Electric Type 3 diesels which worked through from Ipswich to Manchester.

(right) When York first took over haulage of their section of the *NORTH COUNTRY CONTINENTAL* to and from Lincoln, they used a D20 for the first two years and then, from late 1929, D49 class took over. Here D49 No.247 calls at Doncaster with an Up service.

As mentioned in the text, the York portion was detached at Lincoln and from there it was usually hauled north by one of Lincoln's D9's up until 1927 when York shed took responsibility for the Lincoln-York portion. Here D9 No.5113 is seen at Dringhouses in the early 1930's with the York portion.

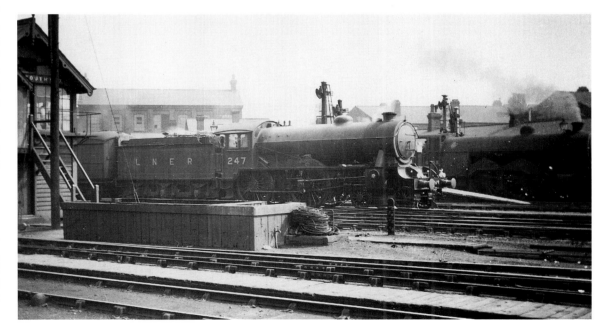

B17 No.2845, seen here at Lincoln, was an Ipswich engine from new in 1935 until October 1941. Working outwards from Ipswich with the *NORTH COUNTRY CONTINENTAL*, the engine would have lost the Birmingham portion at March, and then at Lincoln the York coaches would have been detached leaving the engine with a somewhat lighter load for the arduous climb over Woodhead. The B17 would terminate at Manchester (Central) and the train would then continue on to Liverpool with another engine. Meanwhile the B17 would proceed to Gorton shed for servicing and an overnight stay before retracing its steps back to Ipswich on the next afternoon.

New England C1 No.4407 sets out from York to London with *THE NORSEMAN* in 1931. This Atlantic would work through to King's Cross having just relieved a N.E.Area C7 which had brought the train from Newcastle.

NORWEGIAN BOAT EXPRESS - NORSEMAN - THE NORSEMAN

Newcastle was the port used by passengers to and from Norway who were catered for by two shipping services both of which were Norwegian owned and operated, the B&N Line had sailing's from Newcastle on Mondays, Tuesdays, Thursdays and Saturdays, for which passengers left King's Cross on the 9.50 a.m. Edinburgh express due in Newcastle (Central) at 3.29 p.m. Nothing in the way of boat trains was then needed in either direction as passengers used normal services to and from Newcastle and then needed to make their own way from the station to the quay.

Starting on Saturday 16th June 1928, new facilities nearer the mouth of the river, known as Tyne Commission Quay were used by the ships, and passenger trains could be run right to the side of them. The first through train from King's Cross left that morning at 9.30 a.m. That service, which ran only on Saturdays, did not appear in the public timetable until the issue effective from 9th July 1928, when there were also through coaches on Tuesdays and Thursdays attached to the 10.05 a.m. London to Newcastle express which then ran onwards to the Quay. On Saturday 9th May 1931, the new motor vessel "Venus" made its maiden voyage from the Quay, and in connection with it, from the start of the summer service on 13th June, the LNER began running a special train on Saturdays only at 1.05 p.m. from King's Cross to Tyne Commission Quay which also served the Fred Olsen Line sailing. The LNER also announced that this train would be named *THE NORSEMAN*, carried in that form on the coach roof boards. It quickly became a train of seven corridor coaches and two restaurant cars, not far short of a 350-ton load.

In the 1931 and 1932 summers, New England shed worked this train, and as they did not then have any Pacifics, the Class C1 they used had to be piloted from King's Cross to Peterborough. The additional engine type carried examples of classes C1, C2 and D2 all being noted. New England also worked the train on to York, where their C1 was usually replaced by a C7 class, but occasionally it was a Gateshead Pacific as on 23rd July 1932 when 2598 was used, and was carrying the headboard which had just been provided. Unlike the coach roof boards, this headboard showed only *NORSEMAN*. In the 1933 summer, York shed replaced New England in the working of the train between there and London, which took C7 class engines into King's Cross.

By then the train was becoming so popular that it often needed up to thirteen coaches resulting in a C1 piloting the C7 through to York. So, steps were taken to eliminate this duplication and early in 1934 a start was made on transferring the five Raven Pacifics to York shed. Both 2400 CITY OF NEWCASTLE and 2401 CITY OF KINGSTON UPON HULL worked the 1.05 p.m. out of King's Cross during that summer. In line with North Eastern Area's stubborn aversion to carrying a headboard, these A2 class did not have them and indeed, No.2598 seen with one in July 1932 is the only visual evidence that there was a headboard in the pre-war period.

From the 1935 summer, departure from King's Cross became 12.00 noon, which then continued until 1939 as did haulage by a Pacific. York shed lost the Raven Pacifics through their withdrawal in 1936 and 1937 but were provided with Gresley A1 class in replacement. On the 1938 Bank Holiday

Saturday, I saw their No.2570 hurrying the train north through Doncaster station and from July 1936, both Up and Down trains were limited to boat passengers only. The ignoring of engine headboard also spread to the public timetables but at least the 1939 summer issue showed *THE NORSEMAN* for the Down noon train on Saturdays and in the opposite direction there were two trains with that title both due from Tyne Commission Quay at 1.40 p.m., the Thursday train reaching King's Cross at 7.35 p.m. and the Sunday train with arrival at 8.27 p.m. Then there was a break until the summer of 1946.

On resumption, the timetable mention of the through coaches from London curiously went back to the *NORWEGIAN BOAT EXPRESS* title, and in the final LNER issue, effective from 6th October 1947, there was inclusion of through coaches both from and to London, attached to main line expresses. From London, on Wednesdays and Saturdays only, the 9.30 a.m. Glasgow express took them to Newcastle, from where they were worked to arrive at Tyne Commission Quay at 3.55 p.m. In the Up direction, on Mondays and Fridays only, they left the Quay at 8.55 a.m. to join the 10.00 a.m. from Newcastle and to arrive in King's Cross at 3.30 p.m.

The 1950 summer brought a considerable improvement, as Up and Down boat trains worked through between King's Cross and Tyne Commission Quay again, and their engine carried a new cast headboard with raised letters displaying *THE NORSEMAN*. There was also an appreciable reduction in the running times, and year-round operation was introduced instead of only in summer. Taking the 1954 winter timetable as an example, a

restaurant car train left King's Cross at 9.10 a.m. on Tuesdays and Saturdays with a 2.53 p.m. arrival at the Quay. Only boat passengers could use it including those joining at York which was its only call, although engines had to be changed at Newcastle.

The tortuous journey from Central station to the Quay, which first ran in 1928 was never improved; until September 1938, Class A5/2 tank engines were used, and then Class V1 replaced them. They were still in use on Monday 20th June 1955 when I had the opportunity of being hauled by them. Coming off the "Venus" that Monday morning at 8.40 a.m. we left the Quay behind 67641 up the steeply graded mile to Percy Main North Junction. Halted there for reversal and detachment of that 2-6-2 tank engine whilst 67645 of the same class came on at the other end of the nine-coach train and took us into Newcastle Central station. From the departure at 9.20 a.m., A3 No.60069 carrying the cast headboard showing *THE NORSEMAN* took us non-stop to York and would be into London at 2.17 p.m. By then it was always a Pacific between Newcastle and London and classes A1, A2, A3 and A4 could all be seen on this working.

The last mention of the NORSEMAN appears in the summer 1966 timetable and from then until 2nd May 1970 there was a service between Newcastle Central and Tyne Commission Quay provided by a diesel multiple unit. By then alas, most people went to and from Norway by air.

(above) In North Eastern Area a C7 Atlantic was the more usual motive power up to early 1933, however, during the summer of that year York shed took over responsibility for the train whilst it worked through the Southern Area and the C7's then started to work through to London often with a C1 piloting. This is York's No.706 at Dalton bank on the 31st July 1937 with the Down *NORSEMAN*.

(left) Prior to the Raven Pacifics taking over the workings in 1934, a Gresley Pacific was occasionally supplied for motive power in the N.E.Area. In this 23rd July 1932 view at Croft Spa, Gateshead Pacific No.2598 has charge of the Down train but, more suprisingly that engine is carrying a *NORSEMAN* headboard which, considering the N.E. Area's aversion to locomotive headboards, is a rare sighting hence the inclusion of this none too perfect photograph. the train left King's Cross with D2 No.4330 and C1 No.4406 in charge.

THE NORSEMAN was fully back to pre-war levels of loading in 1950 and Pacific haulage was a daily feature, at least between King's Cross and Newcastle (Central). Here A3 No.60036 COLOMBO of Neville Hill shed carries the first type of BR headboard with raised letters and beaded edges.

Thompson A2/2 No.60502 EARL MARISCHAL, a York Pacific, heads the Up *THE NORSEMAN* at St Neots on 26th July 1952.

(opposite, top) Carrying on the tradition of York shed being responsible for the haulage of *THE NORSEMAN*, Peppercorn A1 No.60140 has the train near Huntingdon on the 19th July 1952.

(opposite, bottom) During the 1950's the A4's also took their turn hauling *THE NORSEMAN* and here 60006 SIR RALPH WEDGWOOD of King's Cross shed approaches York, the train's only stop. Note the additional embellishments on the headboard.

(left) B17 No.2859 in its streamlined guise, and with a new name, heads the *EAST ANGLIAN* in 1937.

(below) Both of the rebuilt and streamlined B17's were released from Doncaster works just a week before the start of the upgraded service from Norwich. The pair were allocated to the shed at Thorpe, taking turns to haul the new six-coach train. Here No.2870 is ready for the midday departure from Norwich to Liverpool Street.

EAST ANGLIAN - THE EAST ANGLIAN

Norwich in the early 1930's was not particularly well connected with London especially through the middle of the day. Taking the February 1932 timetable for example, after 9 a.m. there was a 10.27 a.m. departure which called at all fourteen stations to Ipswich (from where a restaurant car was added) then made calls at Colchester and Chelmsford before arriving in Liverpool Street at 2.04 p.m. On that line there was then nothing until the 2.13 p.m. express which reached London at 4.58 p.m. In the other direction, there was a 5.18 p.m. express from London calling at Chelmsford and Ipswich and due into Norwich at 7.52 p.m. Those unable to catch the 5.18 had to take the 7.10 p.m. via Cambridge and Ely and only reached Norwich at 10.23 p.m. From 1935 the lavish advertising of the streamlined trains must have been gall to Norwich businessmen and required the LNER to make substantial improvement to their service.

The physical characteristics of the Norwich main line did not permit anything similar to *THE SILVER JUBILEE* to be operated but, coinciding with the start of the Leeds high-speed service on 27th September 1937, the Norwich service was also considerably upgraded. On Mondays to Fridays a new train named *EAST ANGLIAN* began and for which six coaches of comparable style to those on the 1937 streamliners were provided. Seating was limited but meals could be served at each place.

It left Norwich at 11.55 a.m. called only at Ipswich and was into London at 2.10 p.m. Return was at 6.40 p.m. with just the Ipswich call and an 8.55 p.m. arrival in Norwich. In September 1938 the journey was cut by five minutes which altered the Norwich times to: out at 12 noon and back at 8.50 p.m. The coaches retained the standard outline and teak panelling with the train name carried on boards at cant rail height. To haul the train, two engines of the 1936/1937 batch of B17 class were fitted with a modified streamline casing, but retained standard green livery. Both were named originally for football clubs, No.2859 being NORWICH CITY and 2870 was TOTTENHAM HOTSPUR.

When No.2859 ran its trials after the streamlined casing was fitted, its curved nameplates and half-football had been removed and replaced by straight plates on the side of the smokebox. Because this broke the football connection, it was thought that Ipswich might feel slighted at the lack of recognition when it was the only other place served by the new train. Their club had not been considered important enough to warrant a "Football" class engine being named Ipswich Town. So, before going into service, No.2859 was renamed EAST ANGLIAN, which covered all eventualities, and No.2870 changed to CITY OF LONDON. As was then usual, on engines having the wedge shape front end, no headboard was provided for the train name. As was the case with the high-speed trains, this service was withdrawn at the outbreak of war on 3rd September 1939, but unlike their stock, the six coaches of the *EAST ANGLIAN* continued to be used on expresses out of Liverpool Street station throughout the war.

After the war ended, this set of six coaches was refurbished and with two other corridor thirds added to them, the *EAST ANGLIAN* began to run again on Monday 7th October 1946. Its timings differed slightly, Norwich being left at 11.40 a.m. with arrival in London at 2.00 p.m. The 6.40 p.m. departure for the return was retained, but Norwich arrival became 9.00 p.m. Although the two B17 streamlined engines were still based at Norwich, the shed there preferred to use the newly built B1 class for the post-war train. With them a headboard was introduced, at first with a single line of white letters on a black background. During 1950, one of the new standard cast headboards was introduced; this had incurved top corners and the train name was in two lines.

In the summer of 1951, British Railways "Britannia" class 4-6-2 engines became available to operate the ex-G.E. main line and as a result, the timetable was recast to give regular departure times throughout the day for the principal expresses. From Norwich *EAST ANGLIAN* then left at 11.45 a.m. and London departure became 6.30 p.m. but the journey times were only 5 minutes less than in 1937. These departure times were then kept to the end of steam. There was one further change to the headboard; from 1953 it carried *THE EAST ANGLIAN* in three lines and small circular plaques were added showing the arms of London and of Norwich.

No.2870 picks up water in 1938. At the outbreak of war in September 1939, the *EAST ANGLIAN* service was withdrawn and the two B17's spent six month's in store but wartime demands, shortages and the realisation that the conflict was to be somewhat elongated, meant that the luxury of storing selective motive power could not be tolerated. The coaching stock remained in use throughout the war period.

Norwich based B1 No.1271 at Liverpool Street engine terminal in 1948 wearing the LNER version of the *EAST ANGLIAN* headboard. Even though the two streamlined B17's were available when the service began again in 1946, Norwich shed preferred to use their newly acquired B1's.

For the reintroduction of the *EAST ANGLIAN* service in October 1946, the original six-coach set was refurbished and two corridor thirds were added to the train. B1 No.61042 has the new cast, two-line headboard, introduced in 1950. This is the Up train just south of Marks Tey on the 24th March 1951.

(opposite) BR Standard No.70036 - representative of the final form of steam motive power - with the final form of headboard for *THE EAST ANGLIAN*. Norwich Trowse, February 1958.

(left) *THE MASTER CUTLER* at North Harrow in October 1947. The Leicester B1 has been nicely turned out complete with headboard.

(below) A3 No.60052 enters Nottingham (Victoria) with *THE MASTER CUTLER* on 21st June 1949. This headboard is the one presented to the LNER in 1947 by the Cutlers Company and superseded the LNER version in 1950.

THE MASTER CUTLER

There was strong competition between the Great Central and the Midland Railways for the London journeys of Sheffield's businessmen, and this was even intensified after they were made components of the London & North Eastern and the London Midland & Scottish Railways respectively. Throughout the 1930's the LNER's morning train left Sheffield (Victoria) at 7.30 a.m. and arrived in Marylebone at 10.40 a.m., the return train left London at 6.20 p.m. and reached Sheffield at 9.38 p.m. None of the trains which ran on the ex-Great Central lines of the LNER were named officially so this pair of important expresses were anonymous almost to the very end of the LNER's existence.

Commencing Monday 6th October 1947 this couple of existing trains were named *THE MASTER CUTLER*; the Up train left Sheffield (Victoria) at 7.40 a.m., called at Nottingham, Leicester and Rugby and reached Marylebone at 11.15 a.m. The return left London at 6.15 p.m. made the same three calls and arrived Sheffield at 10.02 p.m. In the twelve weeks remaining to the LNER, haulage was by the post-war built B1 class, and Leicester shed was responsible for the working.

During 1951 some A3 class returned to work on the G.C. section and Nos.60052, 60058 and 60102 all did duty on *THE MASTER CUTLER*, but surprisingly on one occasion in July 1953, a V2 class belonging to New England shed at Peterborough worked this train. No.60893 was probably in course

of returning to its home shed because it was one of those which had been loaned to the Southern Region in May to the end of June to cover an emergency.

For the inaugural Up train, the Cutlers Company presented the LNER with a stainless steel cast headboard which had polished lettering in relief against a black background. It could well have been a surprise present, because the LNER had prepared their own headboard in the pre-war longer, single line style, but unique in having a short upper portion to carry THE in much smaller letters. That board had the customary Gill sans letters painted black on a white background. It was in use to 1950 but the

Cutlers' present was used to September 1958 when the steam hauled train on the former G.C. line to Marylebone was superseded by a diesel hauled one with Pullman stock which ran to and from King's Cross. That carried the name on a BR style cast plate so the original stainless steel one was given back to the Cutlers Company, who had it mounted for display in their Hall. LNER Chairman Sir Ronald W. Matthews had been a Master Cutler.

Leicester shedded 60052 again but this time only minutes away from Marylebone. Note that lamps have now given way to discs.

(left) Leicester did not always supply a clean B1. Perhaps 61188 is a stand-in for a last minute failure. However, the twelve vehicles comprising *THE MASTER CUTLER* on this day is more than enough for the B1 seen at Wembley Park, 19th September 1949.

(below) What a wonderful sight - two steam locomotives passing on a chilly day. Neasden based A3 60050, complete with another version of the headboard showing coats-of-arms, passes Annesley shedded K3 No.61980 just south of Rugby, circa 1955.

When V2 No.60893 made its surprise debut on *THE MASTER CUTLER* in July 1953, it was carrying a BR standard type cast headboard with raised letters and beaded edges. Notice that THE has larger letters than the other two words whereas it was the other way round with the LNER period headboard. Northwood.

(below) In a classic pose, A3 No.60102 has the more usual nine-coach load under total control on the run into London with the Up train at Harrow in August 1955. Note that the carriage livery is now standardised.

When *THE MASTER CUTLER* changed to diesel power it also changed its conventional rolling stock to Pullman cars. As if in a move to confuse, It also changed its route and London termini. English Electric Type D206 is seen entering King's Cross on 7th October 1958 after its run up the ECML, gained at Retford.

THE HOLIDAY TRAINS

NORFOLK COAST EXPRESS

FIFE COAST EXPRESS

LOTHIAN COAST EXPRESS

SCARBOROUGH FLIER

NORTHERN BELLE

SCOUTS CRUISE

B.L.A. and B.A.O.R. LEAVE TRAINS

NORFOLK COAST EXPRESS

That was the name of a train which the LNER could well have inherited, but did not. From 1907 the GER had been proud to publicise their *NORFOLK COAST EXPRESS* which, each weekday in summer, ran non-stop over the 130 miles between London and North Walsham. There, the twelve-coach train was split, one portion going to Cromer and Sheringham and the other served Mundesley and Overstrand.

There was a corresponding return service to London, but the 1914-1918 war caused the demise of this officially named train. Before the Great Eastern was in any position to re-start operating such an express, it had been "grouped" into the LNER. Curiously, the latter never showed *any* interest in reviving that train.

The short lived *NORFOLK COAST EXPRESS* was a pure Great Eastern Railway affair and during its seven year existence it ran during the summer months only but was very popular usually loading to twelve bogies which was tonnage aplenty for the 'Clauds' which were the mainstay of motive power until the short period when B12's took over. Cecil J.Allen reported that in July 1908 the Down train was made up of thirteen coaches; nine for Cromer and two each to Sheringham and Mundesley. The tare weight was 317 tons.

FIFE COAST EXPRESS

In the summer of 1910, the North British Railway experimented by running a train from Glasgow to the Fife coast stations on Friday afternoons, with a return on Monday mornings. The response was good enough for them to start a weekday service daily in the 1911 summer which then ran until 1914. After the inevitable wartime break, it resumed in 1921, and when first operated by the LNER in the 1923 summer, the morning train was through from Dundee to Glasgow by way of St. Andrews, Crail and Leven. It left Dundee at 6.22 a.m., St. Andrews at 6.50, made seven calls between Crail and Leven, then only at Aberdour to arrive in Glasgow (Queen Street) at 9.41 a.m.

The afternoon return working was more complicated - it left Glasgow at 4.10 p.m. and from the Edinburgh main line, used the spur at Winchburgh Junction to reach Dalmeny where it made a stop not shown in the public timetable. That enabled passengers for Thornton and Cameron Bridge to transfer into another *FIFE COAST EXPRESS* which had left Edinburgh at 4.52 p.m. After calling at Aberdour the train from Glasgow next stopped at Leven, then made the same calls as the morning train as far as Crail, then at St. Andrews, Guard Bridge and Leuchars Junction to finish in Dundee at 7.38 p.m.

The train from Edinburgh missed out Aberdour called at Thornton and also Cameron Bridge, then from Leven, made the same stops twelve minutes after the Glasgow train had done so, and then terminated at Crail. It left that place next morning at 7.25 for an arrival into Waverley at 9.11 a.m. and, although not graced by title in the timetable, the engine did carry an appropriate head board. The shape of this headboard differed from the stepped type used originally which had FIFE above COAST EXPRESS. In LNER days the shape was segmental and had FIFE COAST above EXPRESS. During the 1930's the return train from Edinburgh had another variant in that FIFE COAST EXPRESS was crammed into the top line with CRAIL below it.

During the 1920's and 1930's all these trains were worked by engines allocated to Dundee shed, usually by LNER Class D32 Nos. 9885 and 9886 to which they gave maintenance to make sure of punctuality and reliability. There is need to emphasise that the only correct LNER title was FIFE and not FIFESHIRE, as Cecil J. Allen would have us believe, and as used in *Bradshaw's Guide*. The latter even led the LNER astray for their summer timetable of 1939. That came about when they changed from their hitherto foolscap size to the smaller Bradshaw format, as both were printed by the same Manchester firm, and LNER proof readers missed spotting it. By the 1940 timetable, all except the names of three trains had been dropped, and *FIFE COAST* was one of them.

In the 1939 summer, the morning train started from Crail at 7.05 a.m. and called at all stations to Thornton, then at Kirkcaldy before halting at Dalmeny to divide into its two portions. First away at 8.47, the Edinburgh coaches reached Waverley at 9.03 a.m. The Glasgow coaches left at 8.52, called at Belmont and were into Queen Street at 9.46 a.m. The return working was again more complicated; leaving Glasgow at 4.06 p.m., it called at Polmont and the timetable then showed it as non-stop to Thornton and semi-fast from there, along the main line to Dundee. It did, however, halt at Delmeny from 4.59 to 5.02 to drop the coaches for the coast resorts, which were then taken on by the train which had left Waverley at 4.50 p.m. and whose headboard included CRAIL. The coaches from Glasgow were left at Crail, the others going forward to St. Andrews and then Dundee, which was reached at 8.06 p.m.

Post-war resumption took place from the beginning of April 1949, but only as a St. Andrews to Glasgow working. From St. Andrews at 7.15 a.m., Glasgow arrival was at 9.53 a.m.; the return left Glasgow at 4.07 p.m., to reach St. Andrews at 6.53 p.m. On the coast line only Crail, Anstruther, Elie and Leven were now served. The train now had the benefit of including twin first-class and triplet third class which had been built in 1935 for *THE SILVER JUBILEE* train.

Outside the summer season use on the named train, this luxurious stock was used on a daily through train from Leven to Glasgow and return. At first on the named train, a painted headboard was carried and in line with post-war custom, showed THE FIFE COAST EXPRESS, which was set in two lines. From 1950, a cast plate became available which had raised letters and a beaded edge. This departed from then current practice by omitting the definite article and just had FIFE COAST above EXPRESS. The working was monopolised by B1 class from Dundee shed, those regularly employed being 61292 and 61402. The *FIFE COAST EXPRESS* ran for the last time from 29th June to 5th September 1959, but with the revision of the services from Glasgow to the Fife coast for the 1957 summer, that title was bestowed on the 3.50 p.m. from Glasgow (which then worked out of Buchanan Street station) to St. Andrews, as from the beginning of May.

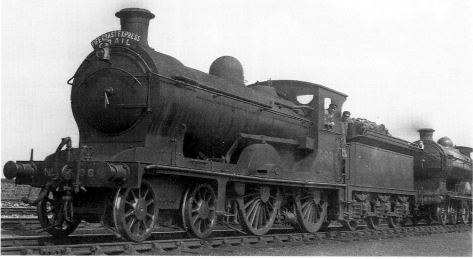

(above) The type of headboard which appeared in early LNER days, this one worn by D32 No.9886 of Dundee shed at Craigentinny sidings.

(left) Also at Craigentinny carriage sidings, D32 No.9885 with yet another headboard which had the extra legend *CRAIL* prominent beneath the main legend. 8th August 1932.

BR period motive power included B1's from Dundee shed and 61402 climbs Cowlairs bank in August 1950 with *THE FIFE COAST EXPRESS*. The headboard is different from the pre-war examples and shows a somewhat conservative use of board. Note the former *SILVER JUBILEE* stock which is by now sans skirts.

(right) B1 No.61292 was a regular Dundee engine working this train and here it carries the last style of headboard with raised letters and beaded edges as it nears Crail.

Dunbar based D29 No.895 heads the *LOTHIAN COAST EXPRESS* at Edinburgh (Waverley) in the year just prior to World War One. When the LNER came into being this express consisted of two portions joined at Longniddry and run to Waverley by a North Berwick shedded C16 tank. From Edinburgh a D30 took the train on to Glasgow. Note the stepped headboard which was used throughout during those first summer's before WW1.

That same headboard was in use when new V1 tank engines took over from the Atlantic tanks east of Edinburgh.

(opposite) West of Edinburgh a different headboard was used by the engine hauling the Glasgow leg. Here D30 No.9424 LADY ROWENA has the train circa 1930 when it was still loading heavily and had just acquired a Pullman restaurant car for the North Berwick portion. The photograph actually depicts the train engine assisting the empty carriages from Queen Street to Cowlairs and is passing under the bridge at Fountainwell Road. By 1935 the *LOTHIAN COAST EXPRESS* was no more, new business trains having replaced it between the coast and Glasgow. Being a summer only service its demise was hardly noticed at the start of the 1935 season.

LOTHIAN COAST EXPRESS

Inaugurated on Monday 3rd June 1912, its period of operation was the Scottish holiday months of June to mid-September. Until 1939, it was a middle-class custom then for families to rent a house at the coast for most of the time that schools were closed, some six to eight weeks, although the head of the family usually had no more than two weeks vacation. So this express provided a service enabling him to extend his stay with the family each evening and night, and still put in reasonable daily hours at his business or profession.

Its first run under the LNER was on 1st June 1923, and for that a set of five coaches had been freshly painted and given L&NER initials. Each weekday, two of them left Gullane at 8.00 a.m. and the other three departed from the North Berwick at 8.05 a.m. to join at Longniddry and then run non-stop to arrive in Edinburgh (Waverley) at 8.45 a.m. There the North Berwick shedded engine was replaced by one from Haymarket shed and the train left at 8.50 non-stop to Glasgow (Queen St) for a 9.50 a.m. arrival. On Mondays to Fridays, the five coaches left Glasgow at 3.50 p.m. stopped in Waverley at 4.50 to 4.55 to change engines, then gave a 5.32 p.m. arrival in North Berwick and 5.33 p.m. at Gullane. That 3.50 express from Glasgow also gave useful relief to the 4.00 p.m. Glasgow-Leeds, always a heavily loaded train. The Glasgow departure on Saturdays was at 12.25 p.m. with a call at Falkirk and a 1.28 p.m. arrival in Edinburgh, then 2.12 p.m. at North Berwick and 2.13 p.m. at Gullane.

Normally, Class C16 4-4-2 tank engines Nos.9448 and 9449 were used by North Berwick shed until the 1931 summer when new Class V1 2-6-2 tank engines took over. On the Gullane branch Class C15 No.9053 was the regular engine. West of Edinburgh it was normal to see a class D30 at the head but the Saturday return train could have a St. Margarets D49 'Shire' as motive power. Instead of the 'Scott' 4-4-0, occasionally used, one of their A1 class Nos.2563 to 2567 and even one of their three ex North Eastern Atlantics No.714 was seen.

The original headboard was of the stepped type with LOTHIAN above COAST EXPRESS, and whilst its use was peculiar to east of Edinburgh, it could still be seen into the 1930's. In LNER days the board which Haymarket shed used was of segmental shape and showed LOTHIAN COAST above EXPRESS.

In 1932, there were two minor changes - the inclusion of a Pullman restaurant car working from and back to North Berwick; the other was the end for the Gullane portion due to the closing of that branch to passengers from 12th September 1932. The named train continued to run in the 1933 and 1934 summers but after September 1934, the name ceased to be used, as did the regular through running between North Berwick and Glasgow. Commencing 1st January 1935, new business trains were introduced between North Berwick and Edinburgh from the coast at 8.25 a.m. and 9.15 a.m., with return services at 5.02 p.m. and 5.48 p.m. with journey times of thirty-one to thirty-four minutes for the 22½ miles. The 1938 summer timetable contained one ghostly reminder of the traffic taken away by the motor car. On Saturdays only the 12.08 p.m. from Glasgow was a through train to North Berwick with arrival at 1.48 p.m. but there was no through train at all in the opposite direction. No wonder that the name *LOTHIAN COAST EXPRESS* had quietly disappeared.

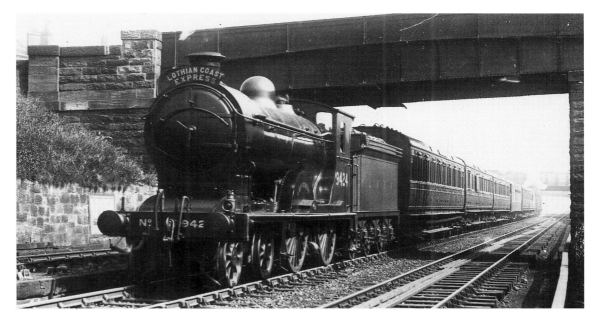

Roof boards had to suffice during the early LNER era of the *SCARBOROUGH FLIER*. Here D21 No.1246 has the train on the York-Scarborough section of its journey and is passing Kirkham Abbey in 1924.

SCARBOROUGH FLIER - THE SCARBOROUGH FLYER

The Great Northern Railway timetable effective from 1st August 1880 for the main line has a column in which "Scarboro' and Whitby Express" is displayed prominently. It left King's Cross at 1.30 a.m. called at Grantham, Newark, Retford and Doncaster and reached York at 2.45 p.m. The North Eastern Railway then took until 4.15 p.m. to get it to Scarborough and the Whitby arrival was at 5.00 p.m. In contrast to the emphasis given to that train two columns ahead of it, the 10 o'clock departure for Edinburgh was simply headed "Spl. Exp" in very small type. There was a corresponding Up train which left Whitby at 9.15 a.m., and Scarborough at 10.45 a.m. to be due into King's Cross at 4.52 p.m.

The GNR's final summer timetable in 1922 included an 11.20 a.m. departure from King's Cross for a "Harrogate, Scarborough and Glasgow Express" with luncheon cars London to Scarborough which made calls at Peterborough, Grantham and Doncaster to arrive in York at 3.21 p.m. and into Scarborough at 4.37 p.m. The return service left Scarborough at 3.00 p.m. and was due into London at 8.10 p.m. and which had 'Dining Car Scarboro' to King's Cross.

So forty-two years had only given that holiday express an eight percent time cut. But the LNER quickly saw the possibilities of traffic growth through holiday visits to Scarborough by Londoners, and in their first summer gave that resort a service in its own right instead of sharing one. The new company did the job properly by introducing a non-stop run to York, 188.2 miles in $3\frac{1}{2}$ hours, and only $4\frac{1}{2}$ hours to Scarborough, a 15% cut on the 1922 timings and, the same applied to the return service. Departures were at 11.50 a.m. from London and at 3.00 p.m. from Scarborough'.

By the 1924 summer, the LNER Advertising Department had begun to flex its muscles and on Monday 14th July announced through the newspapers that the 11.50 a.m. from King's Cross was to be known officially as the *SCARBOROUGH FLIER*. To get a train named was indeed a coup, all the more so one which so concerned the North Eastern Area, and results proved that Scarborough's special treatment was a money-spinner. In 1933, the time to and from York was cut to $3\frac{1}{4}$ hours and then in 1935 to just 3 hours which meant 62.7 m.p.h. start to stop, making it one of the fastest on the LNER until the streamliners were introduced. That was the Mondays to Friday's schedule because for Saturdays in the 1930's capacity had to be augmented considerably. Leaving at 10.50 a.m. an extra train for Scarborough (only) and with restaurant cars, paused only for a change of engine at York and reached Scarborough at 3.00 p.m. The named train left at its normal 11.00 a.m. time, made a call at York to change engine and also to detach Whitby portion and arrived 3.07 p.m. at Scarborough. Then, at 11.25 a.m. a restaurant car train left London for Whitby and that called at Selby to detach a portion for Bridlington. These three Saturday trains had corresponding returns due into King's Cross at 2.25 p.m., 2.35 p.m. and 2.45 p.m. On summer Sundays there was also an 11.15 a.m. from King's Cross to Scarborough and Whitby with 3.56 p.m. and 4.43 p.m. arrivals, and one from Scarborough at 11.40 a.m., due into London at 4.15 p.m. but neither of those qualified for naming. All these trains normally had twelve coaches, often strengthened on Saturdays to fifteen or even sixteen.

From the start of the non-stop running to and from York, haulage by a Pacific was needed and was provided by those shedded at Doncaster, at first A1 then A3 and A4 class being used regularly. After 1939 the *SCARBOROUGH FLIER* did not run for another ten summers. Although named from July 1924, coach roof boards had to suffice until the 1932 summer, when the engine began to carry a headboard and that showed the name in two lines. In 1936, a longer shallower board was provided for use beyond York; that had the name in Gill sans lettering in a single line. It was much more suitable for engines of Darlington design with their lamp iron on the top of the smokebox. Haulage in the N.E. Area was first done by D21 class then by D20's, but in the 1930's usually by a D49, all of them on York shed's roster.

When *THE SCARBOROUGH FLYER* was able to resume running in the 1950 summer from Sunday 4th June it was only on Sundays, Mondays and Saturdays from London and on Mondays, Saturdays and Sundays from Scarborough. At first a refurbished two-line headboard was used between London and York and now had THE on the top line above SCARBOROUGH FLYER. The Up train was now a York shed working and they normally used either a V2 or a Peppercorn A1 class, the train having been brought in from Scarborough by a B1, B16 or a D49 class. Doncaster shed did not now work this train, the Down haulage being done by a King's Cross shedded Pacific or V2. The schedule did not justify the FLYER name (even with its altered spelling) as it took from 11.05 a.m. until 3.52 p.m. for the London-Scarborough journey and from 11.30 to 4.16 in the Up direction.

For the 1952 summer, nineteen minutes were cut from the Down time but the Up time did not benefit and the train only ran to Scarborough on

Fridays and Saturdays, with return on Saturdays and Sundays. By then, the painted headboard had been replaced by a cast plate with beaded edge and raised lettering with each of the three words on a separate line.

As happened to so much holiday passenger traffic, travel by motor car was the cause of progressive decline. In 1953, York shed was no longer bothering to use an engine headboard to and from Scarborough in contrast to the Eastern Region attitude where in late August 1959 the Down train in King's Cross station was headed by an immaculate (and appropriately named) A4 class SEAGULL, complete with headboard. This service continued until the end of the 1962 summer and that was the finale for *THE SCARBOROUGH FLYER.*

Doncaster provided the motive power, usually an A1 or A3 during the pre-war years, for the ECML section of the journey. A1 No.4477 GAY CRUSADER has just backed on to train at York and is ready for the non-stop dash to London.

Still without a headboard, the Up Flier' has one of Doncaster's new A3's, No.2752, for motive power in this June 1929 scene at York.

In 1932 a headboard was at last introduced and another Doncaster A3, No.2751, has charge of the train during the 1938 season.

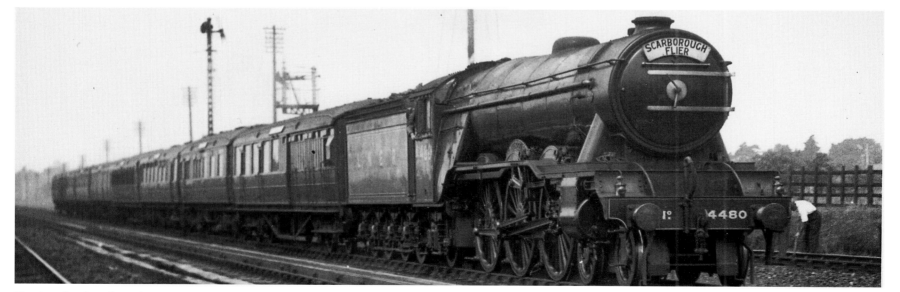

The two-line headboard sat nicely on the top lamp iron of an A3.

For the York-Scarborough section, York shed provided the motive power and especially for their engines, a separate and somewhat different, one-line head board was used. D49 No.288 takes the train on to Scarborough in the late 1930's.

(above) For the post-war resumption of the train in 1949 a new headboard was created and this one had a couple of changes including spelling from the 1932 version - was now *THE SCARBOROUGH FLYER*. Here at Ganwick, newly named and in blue livery, Peppercorn A1 No.60121 has the Up train in the summer of 1950. York shed were responsible for the Up train whilst King's Cross shed provided for the Down train.

(right) Leaving York for the Capital, a rather grubby V2 No.60929 heads the train in 1951.

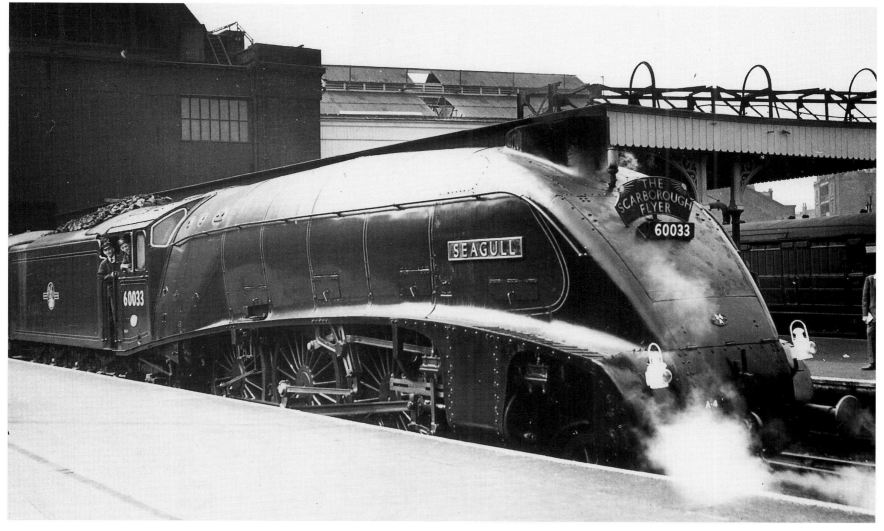

In total contrast to the previous illustration, King's Cross A4 No.60033 SEAGULL presents a wonderful sight at the London terminus in August 1959. At the end of summer 1962 train named *THE SCARBOROUGH FLYER* would evaporate from the timetables and in that same year this locomotive would be condemned.

(opposite) The 'standardised' headboard of 1952 with the wording on three lines in raised letters surrounded by beaded edges. B1 No.61071, of York shed, at Scarborough in June 1954, mirrors the general grubbiness of locomotives at that period.

(left) One of the non-starters for the headboard trials at Doncaster works yard.

(above) The chosen *NORTHERN BELLE* headboard - one line, narrow and acceptable in N.E. Area.

NORTHERN BELLE

History does repeat itself. In the 1930's, sea cruises grew rapidly as an attractive form of holiday and using one of their newly built boats out of Harwich, the LNER found them to be lucrative so the Advertising Department dusted off an idea which had worked almost sixty years previously. In 1878, a private party had hired a Pullman sleeping car and a Pullman parlour car (in which a piano was installed), together with two Midland Railway vans, one of which was fitted out as a kitchen and the other with a bath, for a 26-day rail cruise. Actually it was on this combination that the first meals were cooked and served on a train. Starting from London St. Pancras station, the party went to Matlock, Buxton, Melrose, Edinburgh, on the Burntisland ferry, Perth via Ladybank, Birnam, Killiecrankie, Kingussie, Inverness, Strome Ferry, Dingwall, Thurso, Wick and back to London via Glasgow. In 1933 the LNER recognised the publicity value of emulating this venture and sanctioned the running of a train which must have been a real headache to the operating staff concerned.

At 11.20 p.m. on Friday 16th June 1933, the first *NORTHERN BELLE* left King's Cross for a week-long, 1,873 mile 'cruise' which took in Edinburgh, Aberdeen, Balloch Pier, Fort William, Mallaig, Edinburgh, Melrose, Humshaugh, Newcastle, Barnard Castle, Penrith, Tebay, Saltburn, Gilling, Pickering, Whitby, Scarborough, York, Lincoln, Ely and Cambridge. The train arrived back at King's Cross the following Friday at 7.58 a.m. It carried sixty passengers at £20 each all-inclusive and was comprised of a day portion of brake first, third sleeper (for train staff), kitchen car, two open firsts, hairdressing saloon/buffet car and a corridor first. The night portion had six of the latest first class sleeping cars and a bogie brake van which provided individual lockers for each passenger's luggage. The cruise was repeated a week later - as planned - but so many applied that it was run again in August.

The working programme contained precise instructions on use of headboards. Two would be provided one for the engine, and a spare in the train. The engine headboard was to be carried throughout but when the train was divided, only the portion conveying passengers was to carry it. The boards were a new shape, following trials of five different ones in Doncaster works yard, longer but less deep, and with the name in a single line in Gill sans letters.

In case the £20 total cost is considered to be ridiculously low, it should be compared with the estimated costs of operating the 'cruise' as set out in a report dated 13th April 1933, as seen in table 1.

Table 1.

Motive Power	£220. 7s. 0d
Guard	£ 14. 2s. 7d
Supervisor	£ 10. 0s. 0d
Restaurant Car Staff	£ 23.10s. 0d
Buffet & Hairdressing Staff	£ 12. 0s. 0d
Sleeping Car Attendants	£ 31. 5s. 6d
Chambermaids	£ 6. 5s. 0d
Cleaners	£ 15. 8s. 6d

Food for train staff (24) estimated by the Hotel Superintendent's representative for the round trip at 15 shillings per head.

The 1,873 miles were made up of 1,581 miles loaded and 292 miles empty, of which about 656 miles would need double-heading. Most of the latter was in Scottish Area where a C11 and D11 worked Edinburgh to Aberdeen and back, two D11's Edinburgh to Balloch Pier and back to Dumbarton (they detached at Balloch Down Starting Signal and propelled the train to the platform at the Pier), from Dumbarton to Mallaig and back two D34's were rostered, then from Cowlairs East Junction one D11 took the train to Corstophine for the overnight stop there. From there, a K2 and a J39 were used over the Waverley Route and the Boarder Counties line through to Newcastle. In the North Eastern Area, the train was largely in the care of K3 and D49 classes, although they made some use of J21 class for hauling the night portion when it ran empty and separately.

By 1934, four 'cruises' were run, all starting in June, and that became the regular pattern until the 1939 summer, after which they were never resumed. When C11 class were withdrawn, train-brake fitted J37's took their place and in 1938 and 1939 on the West Highland Line, use was made of the new K4 class built specially for that line.

How the headboard looked on an A3 - well almost. This is No.2751, which was at that time in 1933 carrying out smoke clearance tests and with the top portion of its smokebox cut away it had to wear the board just above mid-way. HUMORIST is arriving in King's Cross with the returning 'Cruise' train in June 1933.

(opposite) The variety of motive power used for the 'Cruise' was impressive - besides express passenger and mixed traffic engines a number of goods engines were also involved.

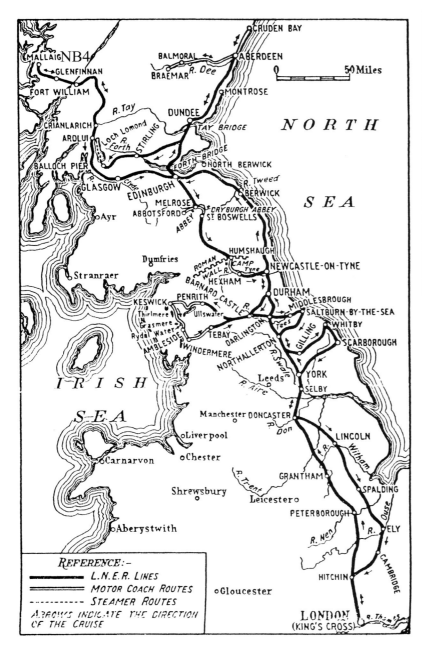

The train was often split which made it more manageable over some of the difficult stretches of line. Here is the 'day' section of the 'Cruise' with two locomotives each having a headboard.

(opposite, top) Plan of the LNER train used on the *NORTHERN BELLE*.

(opposite, bottom) In the last two years before war, newly built K4's were used on the West Highland line.

(left) The route of the *NORTHERN BELLE* cruise as published in the June 23rd edition of *Railway Gazette*.

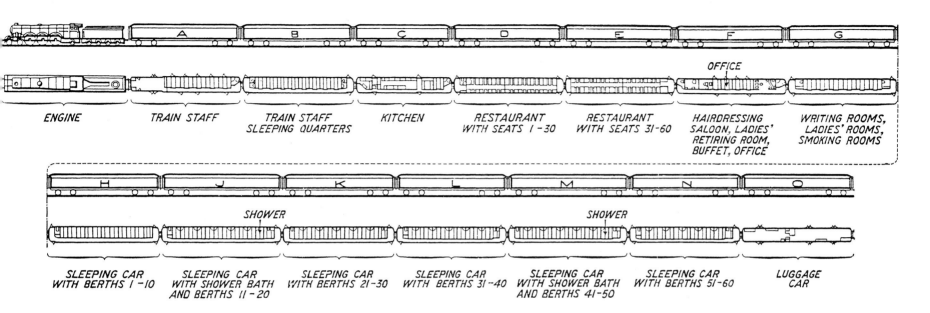

| ENGINE | TRAIN STAFF | TRAIN STAFF SLEEPING QUARTERS | KITCHEN | RESTAURANT WITH SEATS 1 - 30 | RESTAURANT WITH SEATS 31-60 | HAIRDRESSING SALOON, LADIES' RETIRING ROOM, BUFFET, OFFICE | WRITING ROOMS, LADIES' ROOMS, SMOKING ROOMS |

| SLEEPING CAR WITH BERTHS 1 -10 | SLEEPING CAR WITH SHOWER BATH AND BERTHS 11 - 20 | SLEEPING CAR WITH BERTHS 21 - 30 | SLEEPING CAR WITH BERTHS 31 -40 | SLEEPING CAR WITH SHOWER BATH AND BERTHS 41-50 | SLEEPING CAR WITH BERTHS 51-60 | LUGGAGE CAR |

(above) This J37-D11 combination, 9008 and 6397, have the complete train at Perth. Note only one headboard is in use on this occasion.

(right) Two D11's take their turn with the *NORTHERN BELLE*.

(opposite) Two D34's usually headed the section from Dumbarton to Mallaig and return. Here D34 No.9035 is at Mallaig harbour with an unidentified 4-4-0.

A J39 and K2 were rostered for the Waverley route section of the first 'Cruise'.

(left) Another York K3 in charge at Barnard Castle.

(opposite) An unidentified J21 heads what appears to be a night portion of the 'Cruise' at Darlington. Although empty stock portions of the *NORTHERN BELLE* were not supposed to carry headboards, this was not the case here - perhaps the only time a J21 had worn a headboard ?

(left) Two immaculate D49's handled the Darlington to Saltburn stage.

(below) Back on the East Coast main line, the *NORTHERN BELLE* is in the hands of an A3 Pacific. On this day, 24th June 1938, the train ex King's Cross at 7.50 p.m., is near Potters Bar en route for Aberdeen.

(opposite) The *NORTHERN BELLE* did good business for the LNER up to 1939 and here we see A4 No.4467 taking a 'Cruise' out of King's Cross, during daylight at 7.50 p.m., on the first leg of its week long journey.

The annual *SCOUTS CRUISE* had a headboard from its first outing in 1935 and this continued to be displayed throughout the trains five year existence. Here York A1 No.2570 returns the Boy Scouts back to London after their Sunday parade and service at St Olave's church in York on the 5th May 1935.

SCOUTS CRUISE

Another cruise train first ran in 1935, with a headboard of the shape used for the *NORTHERN BELLE*, and showing *SCOUTS CRUISE*. This train was a joint effort between the Boy Scouts Association's newspaper and the LNER. The train left King's Cross to a ceremonial send-off at 8.15 p.m. on Sunday 28th April, carrying 120 Scouts whose home it would be for a week. A nice gesture was the engine chosen to haul it, No.2750 PAPYRUS with Driver Cutteridge, fresh from their record-breaking Newcastle run on which 108 m.p.h. had been reached.

The train ran main line overnight to Leith so that Monday could be spent in Edinburgh, and during that night, it went to Banavie on the Fort William-Mallaig line to provide for climbing and hiking in the Ben Nevis area. On Thursday there was a day journey to Humshaugh (near the Roman Wall) to enable the Scouts to have an evening camp fire on the same spot as the first one which had been lit by their founder Baden Powell in 1908. Rejoining the train, they went to Newcastle for the night, spending Friday in that city and cruising on the Tyne. Early on Saturday the train went to York for a morning visit to the Queen Street railway museum and to spend the rest of the day in and around the city. On Sunday morning they were joined by York Scouts for church parade at St. Olave's and then took the train back to King's Cross, hauled - as they had started - by a Gresley Pacific.

That cruise was repeated each year to and including, 1939; for the LNER it was a useful rehearsal for running the *NORTHERN BELLE*.

On a late April departure from York, this time under more typical skies, the *SCOUTS CRUISE* returns to London behind an A1.

B.L.A. LEAVE TRAIN - B.A.O.R. LEAVE TRAINS

Following the defeat of Germany, British troops in considerable numbers were stationed there for many years and were known as the British Army of the Rhine and also as the British Liberation Army. Arrangements for home leave had to be organised for the service personnel and starting 16th October 1945, and every day thereafter, a ship left Cuxhaven for Hull carrying about 1,400 of them. The ships used needed a minimum twenty-one feet of water and so they had to berth in King George Dock, Hull, where their arrival time was governed by the tide. After the troops disembarked a fleet of Army lorries took them to Paragon station from where special trains ran, one each to London, Manchester and Edinburgh, and which on the first day left at 1.15 p.m., 1.25 p.m. and 3.00 p.m. respectively.

North Eastern Area had still not lost their aversion to naming trains and all those that Hull despatched ran anonymously. The pre-war Riverside Quay facilities at Hull needed alteration to cope with the draught of the ships being used which were the "Empire Rapier", "Empire Cutlass", "Empire Halberd" and "Empire Spearhead", all 7,000 tons war-time built Liberty type. Adequate draught for them at all states of tide was provided by the same devise as that used so successfully for the invasion of Normandy, the artificially created Mulberry harbour. That had not needed all the pontoons which had been built to cover possible losses, so two of the spares still on the English side of the Channel were towed to Hull and moored off Riverside Quay, but with gangways connected to it. Using the outer face of the pontoons for berthing the ships then always had a minimum twenty-one feet of water available and regular arrival and departure times could be established.

The ships were transferred from King George Dock to the improvised Riverside Quay on 16th August 1946 and the trains were then able to leave from tracks on that quay. Buildings on it had been destroyed by bombs during the heavy air raids of early May 1941 but the tracks were intact facilities were easily provided for entering coaches from rail level. Between October 1945 and the end of 1946, Hull dealt with 120,000 troops each way and also had embarked 38,000 German prisoners of war being repatriated. None of the trains were marked.

Significant as was this traffic through Hull, it paled beside what the LNER dealt with through Harwich. On 3rd June 1946, Liverpool Street's Stationmaster greeted the arrival there of the millionth soldier coming on leave. But in addition to those to and through London, thousands needed to go north and west from Parkeston Quay, and a train at 9.40 a.m. took them to Peterborough. Parkeston shed had the working to Ely where March men took it forward.

Known to those concerned as the North Country Troop Special, this was unofficial and no engine headboard was carried and naturally it had no place in the public timetables. As distinct from N.E. the Southern Area were accustomed to using headboards and provided one of standard type with *B.L.A. LEAVE TRAIN* in two lines of white lettering on a black background. From Peterborough these trains often went north on the main line behind an A4 streamlined engine duly carrying the headboard. Whilst this traffic continued for some years, curiously it seems to have almost completely evaded enthusiastic photographers. The B.L.A. (British Liberation Army) title soon changed to B.A.O.R. (British Army of the Rhine).

B.A.O.R. LEAVE TRAINS

The first of these trains ran in late 1945 as specials and the troops were brought to Harwich by the LNER's own ship, S.S. "Antwerp", the GWR's S.S. "St Helier", the Burns-Laird line's M.V. "Royal Ulsterman" and the former LNER S.S. "Vienna" which the Government had taken over in 1941.

By the beginning of 1946, a regular service through Parkeston Quay West had been established and in addition to the "Vienna" the boats were "Empire Parkeston" and "Empire Wansbeck". The trains left at 8.00 a.m. and 8.50 a.m. from Parkeston Quay West and the return times were 2.18 p.m. and 3.00 p.m. from London (Liverpool Street). Until almost the end of 1946 normal haulage was shared by class B12/3 from Stratford and Parkeston's B17's. The latter were replaced by B1 class, transferred to Parkeston and which became the regular engines. No engine headboard was provided for them.

Until 26th September 1961 these leave trains continued to operate, but the users of them were then switched to the normal boat trains, the traffic being reduced considerably by married quarters having been provided in Germany for service personnel.

The WTT for the winter of 1958/59 had three trains each way on Tuesdays, Thursdays and Saturdays from Parkeston Quay West at 8.50 a.m., 9.35 a.m., and 9.55 a.m. with returns from Liverpool St. on Mondays, Wednesdays and Fridays at 7.40 p.m., 8.13 p.m., and 8.47 p.m. each train a set of nine coaches, rostered just to this service but of varied composition. The 8.50 a.m. and 8.47 p.m. return provided for 84 (1st) and 376 (2nd) class seats, the 9.35 a.m. and 8.13 p.m. return had 42 (1st) and 432 (2nd), whilst the 9.55 a.m. and 7.40 p.m. return catered for 57 (1st) and 408 (2nd), so the daily seat total was 1,399 in both directions. These trains understandably did not appear in the public timetables and no engine headboard was ever carried.

Peterborough, a group of soldiers and the Station Master stand alongside the *B.L.A. LEAVE TRAIN* with A4 No.4494 ready for the journey northwards in 1946.

OFFICIALLY NAMELESS

PORTS TO PORTS EXPRESS

ABERDEEN-PENZANCE SERVICE

GARDEN CITIES & CAMBRIDGE BUFFET EXPRESS

The *PORTS TO PORTS EXPRESS* southbound from Sheffield to Banbury in the mid 1920's hauled by a Leicester based former GCR Atlantic No.5267.

PORTS TO PORTS EXPRESS

Widely known by this title, the name was never given official recognition, nor was it used in timetables. The service began on 1st May 1906 when the North Eastern, Great Central and Great Western Railways combined to run a through train each way between Newcastle and Cardiff. The main object was to cater for merchant seamen travelling between ships in the Tyne and South Wales ports of Newport, Cardiff and beyond. It proved so useful that from 1st August of the same year it was extended to Barry and commencing 1st July 1909 a through coach was added to connect Hull and Barry. The 1914 war caused the service to be withdrawn but when resumed after the war it was extended to Swansea, a journey of 396 miles from Newcastle. In South Wales it was also diverted slightly to service Penarth docks.

When the LNER took over operation from the Great Central and the North Eastern, the Newcastle departure was at 9.30 a.m. with a 6.40 p.m. arrival at Cardiff and 8.45 p.m. at Swansea. In the opposite direction, the 7.30 a.m. start from Swansea terminated in Newcastle at 6.45 p.m. The Hull through coach was restored from Saturday 12th July 1924 and arrived there at 4.45 p.m., and left the following morning at 10.50 a.m. to join the main train at Sheffield (Victoria). In the 1939 summer, the southbound train left Newcastle at 9.30 a.m., Hull at 10.35 a.m. and reached Swansea at 8.45 p.m. In the other direction, Swansea departure was at 8.15 a.m. with a 4.45 p.m. arrival in Hull and 6.15 p.m. in Newcastle.

Between Newcastle and York the engines used were normally C7 class Atlantics. On the York, and Hull to Sheffield sections, a 4-4-0 was usual, a D20 until the 'Shires' and 'Hunts' took over in the 1930's. On the Sheffield to Banbury section (south of which was Great Western Railway responsibility), a Great Central built C4 class Atlantic was normal motive power, although in the later 1930's it could be a Gresley B17. In 1937, when more of the latter class had been built, Nos.2863, 2864 and 2865 went new to Sheffield, and often were on the 4.45 p.m. into Hull, where previously a D9 and then a D10 had been used.

The train was a 6-coach set including a restaurant car with an extra composite coach for Hull. On alternate days the LNER and the GWR provided the stock on which roof boards showed just the major places served. As happened in 1914, so in 1939 war caused withdrawal of the train.

Restoration of the Newcastle-Swansea, but not the Hull portion, was made in October 1946, and the Great Western changed the route they operated, using Oxford, Swindon and the Severn Tunnel instead of via Cheltenham and Gloucester. Their set of six coaches were of the type with end doors and each had roof boards showing the major places served. The LNER six-coach set had roof boards only on the two end coaches, and simply showed Newcastle - Swansea. The former Great Central and North Eastern Atlantic type engines were almost life expired by now and south of York a Thompson B1 did the job whilst V2's were usually in charge north of York. It was soon clear that the traffic pattern had altered appreciably to be no longer viable and this service was redundant so it was not even included in the final timetable issued by the LNER.

Travelling on the Aberdeen-Penzance service was certainly an interesting if exhausting experience. Here the return coaches are on the front of this Edinburgh to Aberdeen train hauled by former NBR Atlantic No.9874 on its journey through Fife.

ABERDEEN - PENZANCE SERVICE

Monday 3rd October 1921 saw the start of the longest through journey that the ordinary person could make in Great Britain, one of 785 miles between Aberdeen and Penzance. Only very dedicated enthusiasts made the full trip, which was by through coaches and not a separate train. It was both longer and quicker than the 722 miles done by the "Jellicoe" specials which ran regularly during the 1914-1918 and 1939-1945 wars and during those periods carried more than a million of troops on that wearisome journey.

To start this service needed the co-operation of four major independent railways, North British, North Eastern, Great Central and Great Western. It comprised of either one (or occasionally two) coaches for 1st and 3rd classes of corridor type. Provided originally by the North British and the Great Western, that of the former became London & North Eastern Railway responsibility from the Grouping of Monday 1st January 1923. In their various trains, these coaches could readily be identified by their long roof boards which displayed the extent of the journey.

The through coaches made use of existing main line trains between Aberdeen and York also Swindon and Penzance. To link them , the Great Central put on a new express from York to Swindon via Sheffield, Nottingham, Leicester and Banbury. In 1923, when the LNER took over, the southbound coaches left Aberdeen at 9.45 a.m. on a restaurant car express to Edinburgh, reached at 1.15 p.m. They went forward at 1.30 p.m. on a London bound train from which they were detached at York, where they arrived at 6.04 p.m. The link train left at 6.25 p.m. non-stop to Sheffield (Victoria) using the Knottingley and Swinton Joint line, which brought the Lancashire & Yorkshire (and from 1923 the LMS) into indirect concern. Calling only at Nottingham (Victoria), Leicester (Central) and Rugby, the coaches were handed over to the Great Western in Banbury at 10.00 p.m., and with just a call at Oxford, arrived in Swindon at 11.30 p.m. There the coaches were attached to the sleeping car express which had left Paddington at 10.00 p.m. and which took them through to a 7.26 a.m. arrival next morning in Penzance. If desired, passengers could secure a sleeping berth from Swindon by notifying any stationmaster en route before 3.00 p.m. on the day required.

Going north, Penzance was left at 11.00 a.m. with a Luncheon and Tea Car express for London from which it was detached at Westbury at 5.06 p.m. The coach(es) worked forward as a special to arrive Swindon at 6.05 p.m. Departure was at 6.15 p.m., there was a call at Oxford, and the LNER took over on 7.37 p.m. arrival at Banbury. On the ex-Great Central, the same calls were made before the York arrival at 11.13 p.m. There it was retained until the 1.09 a.m. departure of the 8.25 p.m. sleeping car express from King's Cross to Edinburgh, due there at 7.32 a.m.

The coach went forward on the 7.40 a.m. express from Edinburgh to Aberdeen where its journey ended at 11.22 a.m. With prior notice, a sleeping berth could be obtained from York. In the 1939 summer, Aberdeen departure was at 10.20 a.m., Edinburgh was left at 2.05 p.m. and York at 6.22 p.m. to arrive Swindon at 11.32 p.m. and Penzance at 7.25 a.m. next morning. In the other direction, Penzance was left at 10.45 a.m., Swindon at 6.15 p.m. to arrive in York at 11.33 p.m. The previous lengthy lay-over had been eliminated as departure was at 11.50 p.m. which gave arrival in Edinburgh at 4.00 a.m. next morning and into Aberdeen at 11.09 a.m.

Dependence on such connections as this working involved was out of the question under war conditions, so the lengthy through run had to be cancelled, but the York - Swindon leg was maintained in its own right throughout the war. Post-war it was recognised how few really needed the full journey, so the through coaches were not restored, much of their facility being covered by through trains between Edinburgh and Plymouth in both directions.

Cambridge shedded C1, No.4440, blasts out of the city with the 3.30 p.m. train in March 1938. By now the five times each way, daily 'Beer Trains' were loading up to ten coaches for the one hour and twelve minute journey.

GARDEN CITIES & CAMBRIDGE BUFFET EXPRESSES

Until May 1932, the accepted way for Cambridge-London travel was the 55³/₄ miles to and from Liverpool Street, on which the quickest train took 78 minutes. Via Hitchin it was 58 miles to King's Cross a route probably offering better punctuality due to less congestion in the London suburban area.

Commencing Monday 2nd May 1932, five new fast trains began running on the ex-G.N. line and in the third class corridor coaches, three aside seating with armrests was introduced. An open buffet car for meals and drinks was included and as calls were made at Welwyn Garden City and Letchworth, these trains were given the name *GARDEN CITIES AND CAMBRIDGE BUFFET EXPRESS*. They were so indicated by roof boards on the buffet car and in the timetables but it must have been too cumbersome to put on an engine headboard because these were never carried. At first, running times were similar to those to and from Liverpool Street, but within a year were cut to a best time of 72 minutes. The five trains were spread over the day, Cambridge departures being at 9.25 a.m., 12.30 p.m., 3.25 p.m., 5.25 p.m. and 10.10 p.m. From King's Cross they were 9.35 a.m., 12.40 p.m., 2.10 p.m., 8.10 p.m. and 9.55 p.m. They proved so popular that loads soon grew to eight and even up to ten coaches. Undergraduates found the buffet car a great attraction and quickly dubbed this service the "Beer Trains".

The trains were worked by engines mainly shedded at Cambridge, usually of C1 class which were of course part of the normal scenery at King's Cross station, and as far out as Hitchin. But on occasion, an interesting variety of classes were pressed into service including B12, B17, C4 and D16, all of which had to work hard on the eight miles of 1 in 200 up to Potters Bar in order to cover the 20.3

miles to stop at Welwyn Garden City in twenty-five minutes from King's Cross.

From September 1939 war conditions put a stop to this enterprise but by the end of the LNER, four trains each way had been restored albeit with slightly different departure times. Wartime arrears of maintenance to the track also militated against the sprightly running of pre-war, and only one of the trains was scheduled to be as quick as 82 minutes. Much of the haulage was now done by B17, but more especially by the Thompson B1 class. The train name had also been simplified to just *CAMBRIDGE BUFFET EXPRESS* and from October 1950 an effort was made to systemise departure times. From Cambridge these were 9.10 a.m., 12.10 p.m., 3.10 p.m. and 6.10 p.m.; from King's Cross they were 9.02 a.m., 12.05 p.m., 2.05 p.m. and 8.05 p.m.

By September 1954 the regular times past the hour had been abandoned, those from Cambridge becoming 9.18 a.m. and 11.10 a.m. then 3.15 p.m. and 6.12 p.m., whilst those from King's Cross were 9.22 a.m. and 11.53 a.m. then 2.05 and 8.02 p.m. The best time, by just one train was eighty minutes.

When the final Bradshaw was published in May 1961, there were again five Cambridge Buffet Expresses each way, but none of them managed better than eighty-six minutes from Cambridge and eighty-eight minutes from King's Cross. Cambridge departures were at 9.15 a.m. and 11.15 a.m., 1.15 p.m., 3.15 p.m. and 5.57 p.m., and from London at 9.05 a.m., 11.05 a.m., 1.05 p.m., 3.05 p.m. and 7.55 p.m. Why just the last one each way broke the systematic departure times is unknown but typifies the uncaring attitude so often taken by British Railways' officials to their paying customers. Those out-of-sequence (and earlier) departures must have caused many people to miss them, to their chagrin - and considerable inconvenience.

C1 No.4439 heads a five vehicle 'Beer Train' at Cambridge in 1932.

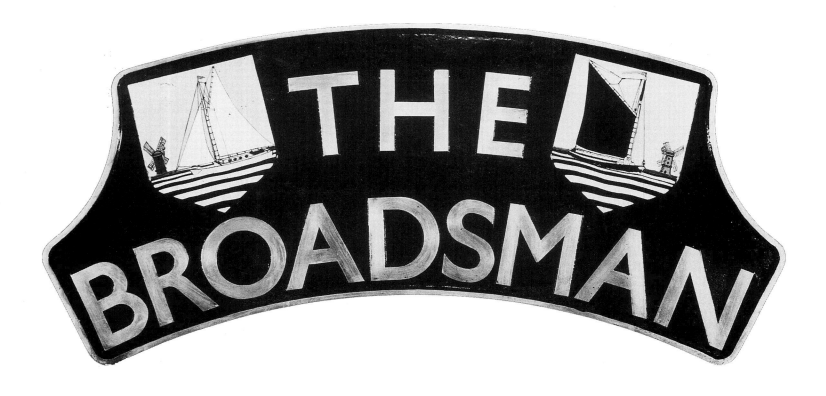

DEVELOPMENTS BY BRITISH RAILWAYS

The 1948 summer services began on 31st May with two encouraging features, *FLYING SCOTSMAN* resumed non-stop running (*see* Part I)and another new named train started on the former GCR mainline. On that day, the 10.00 a.m. from Bradford (Exchange) to Marylebone became *THE SOUTH YORKSHIREMAN* and to complement it in the Down direction, that name was carried by a new service from Marylebone at 4.50 p.m. The headboards for this train (which were carried until the service ceased on 2nd January 1960) also introduced a new shape and style which set the standard for all subsequent headboards. The style derived from the special stainless steel type used on *THE MASTER CUTLER* and the shape followed that of the July 1947 board which was made for *THE DAY CONTINENTAL* but became deep enough for three lines of lettering where required. Instead of a thin steel plate with painted lettering, there was now a casting with a beaded edge and integral lettering in relief. Edges and letters were usually bright metal and showed up well against the painted black background.

THE SOUTH YORKSHIREMAN

TEES-TYNE PULLMAN

THE NORFOLKMAN

THE CAPITALS LIMITED

THE ELIZABETHAN

THE WHITE ROSE

THE WEST RIDING

THE FENMAN

THE NORTHUMBRIAN

THE NORTH BRITON

THE TYNESIDER

THE EASTERLING

THE BROADSMAN

THE HEART OF MIDLOTHIAN

THE TALISMAN

THE FAIR MAID

THE ESSEX COAST EXPRESS

THE TEES-THAMES

ANGLO-SCOTTISH CAR CARRIER

THE SOUTH YORKSHIREMAN had regular Pacific haulage between 1949 and 1957 when V2's took over for the last couple of years before abandonment of the service. Here, in September 1949, 60048 is near Northwick Park.

THE SOUTH YORKSHIREMAN

British Railways were even more favourably inclined towards train naming then the LNER, and as early as 31st May 1948 they introduced *THE SOUTH YORKSHIREMAN*. This continued the long-established express service which the Lancashire & Yorkshire and Great Central Railways had operated, leaving Bradford (Exchange) around 10 o'clock, and returning from Marylebone as the 6.20 p.m. Because *THE MASTER CUTLER* had taken over that return time, the Bradford train in turn superseded, as far as the Penistone call, on what had been the pre-war 4.55 p.m. express from Marylebone to Manchester. In neither direction however, did *THE SOUTH YORKSHIREMAN* emulate the glory days of the ex-Great Central Atlantics and 'Directors' on the pre-war equivalents.

On that last day of May 1948, the Up named train left Bradford (Exchange) at 10.00 a.m. behind a former LMS Class 5 which called at Huddersfield, and then took it through Penistone to Sheffield (Victoria). Thence, a B1 hauled it to Leicester where another of the same class took over to get it into Marylebone at 3.30 p.m. The return departed from there at 4.55 p.m. and initially it had a diversion to call at Chesterfield before an 8.42 p.m. arrival in Sheffield. That did not attract the traffic expected so was soon altered for the train to continue on the main line and reach Sheffield at 8.26 p.m.

In Victoria, three of the coaches and the two restaurant cars finished their day's work and were detached. The other five coaches went on to call at Penistone, Huddersfield and then terminate in Bradford at 10.20 p.m. hauled by the Class 5. One benefit of Nationalisation accrued in that the ex-LMS engine which had worked the morning train from Bradford was no longer laid over in Sheffield all day awaiting the evening return working. Instead, it took a York-Bournemouth to Leicester and returned with a Bournemouth train in ample time to work the named train back to Bradford and both ways on that section, carried a headboard. That headboard was both a new shape and style, being a cast plate with beaded edge and raised letters the plate having incurved top corners. The name was in two lines, THE SOUTH superimposed on YORKSHIREMAN. On its trip to and from Leicester, the plate was carried by the Class 5, but reversed.

Between Bradford and Huddersfield (each way) the route was through the Spen Valley and conditional calls could be arranged at Cleckheaton, Liversedge and Heckmondwike but by June 1953, more lucrative traffic was obtained by diverting it to call at Halifax and then go via Brighouse to Huddersfield. That made only a slight difference to the arrival times which then became 3.29 p.m. into London and 10.17 p.m. into Bradford.

Getting new Peppercorn A1 class in 1949, GN line sheds could spare some A3's to go and deal with the heavier trains on the GC line, so in February 1949, Leicester shed got Nos. 60048, 60049, 60052, 60053 and 60061 to use to and from London and *THE SOUTH YORKSHIREMAN* became one of their regular duties. By September 1957, when 60049 left, all the A3's had returned to ex GN sheds, V2 class replacing them.

In 1958, the ex GC line was transferred from Eastern Region to London Midland Region control and a gradual running down of passenger services began. Then, from 2nd January 1960, all express services on it ceased so that was the end for *THE SOUTH YORKSHIREMAN*.

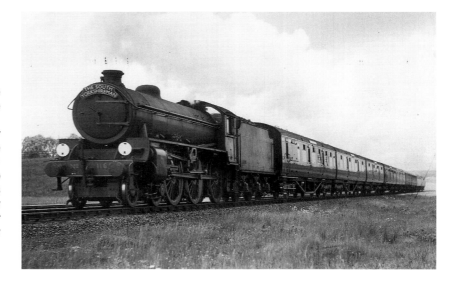

From Sheffield, at the start of the service, the nine coach train had B1 haulage to Leicester where engines were changed - another B1 took the train onto Marylebone. This is No.1161 with the very first Up train near Ruddington, 31st May 1948.

Heaton based A3 No.60069 heads the Up *TEES-TYNE PULLMAN* at Ganwick on 30th September 1948. On this date the train consisted eight vehicles.

Another Heaton based Pacific, this time the still unnamed Peppercorn A1 No.60116, heads the Up nine-coach consist in April 1949 at Marshmoor.

Pressed into use because of the failure of the booked Pacific, Thompson B1 No.61097 of Hitchin shed finds the eight-coach load of the UP train easily within its limits. Potters Bar, 21st August 1953.

TEES-TYNE PULLMAN

This train began running on 27th September 1948 to try and recover the lucrative traffic which *THE SILVER JUBILEE* had generated in 1935-1939 as the first streamlined train. The new Pullman could not match that train's 4-hour timing as the track was not yet back to pre-war standard, but it left Newcastle at 9.00 a.m. called only at Darlington and reached London at 2.16 p.m. The Jubilee's return time of 5.30 p.m. was kept, but it was 10.50 p.m. when it arrived in Newcastle.

With improvement in track maintenance, from 23rd May 1949, both journeys were cut to 5 hours and to give more acceptable arrival times, the departure time from London was exchanged with that of *THE YORKSHIRE PULLMAN* and then became 4.45 p.m., to arrive Darlington at 8.56 p.m. and 9.40 p.m. at Newcastle. From 25th September 1949 another five minutes Up, and eight minutes Down were cut out. In May 1961 it left Newcastle at 9.25 a.m. and Darlington at 10.11 a.m. to reach King's Cross at 2.16 p.m. and returned at 4.50 p.m., to arrive Darlington at 8.57 p.m. and Newcastle at 9.41 p.m. In that direction (only) it called in York at 8.09 p.m. By then it was usually diesel hauled.

The name was carried on a cast headboard, but of the alternative standard 10 in. instead of $14^3/_8$, in. deep and without incurved top corners, in two lines, without THE being included. It was a regular eight or nine car train, invariably hauled by a Pacific type locomotive.

Even with A4 haulage and a load of eight vehicles, this Pullman train could not match the pre-war timings of *THE SILVER JUBILEE*, taking an hour longer for the Newcastle to London journey. No.60025 FALCON was a King's Cross engine

THE NORFOLKMAN

This named train was introduced on 27th September 1948 to complement THE EAST ANGLIAN, to give a morning departure from London and, a late afternoon return from Norwich. From Liverpool Street at 10.00 a.m. and calling only at Ipswich, it arrived Norwich at 12.20 p.m. and returned at 5.00 p.m. to reach London at 7.20 p.m.

Starting with the 1949 summer service, it further justified its county title by going on to Wroxham, North Walsham and Cromer, the return train making those same stops. In effect, it resembled the GER's *NORFOLK COAST EXPRESS* which the 1914-1918 war had killed off and the LNER had never managed to restart.

From 1948 to 1951 the eight coaches were normally hauled between London and Norwich by class B1's from Stratford shed and after the Norwich reversal, by a V1 class 2-6-2 tank to and from Cromer. Interactive variations from the B1 were trails in May 1949 of a Southern Region 'Battle of Britain' Class Pacific, No.34059 SIR ARCHIBALD SINCLAIR, on loan, also on Tuesday 12th April 1949, Class B12/3 No.61556 took over at Colchester after a B1 failure. Then from 1st February 1951 this working was handed over to B.R. Standard 'Britannia' Pacifics.

(opposite) The inaugural train about to depart from Liverpool Street on Monday 27th September 1948. The Stratford B1, which had been especially 'bulled-up' for this occasion, still had its LNER number. Until the advent of the 'Britannia' Pacifics in 1951, Stratford's B1's continued to monopolise the train. Note the BR standard cast headboard is yet to appear.

There was a minor change from Monday 20th September 1954, when Cromer (High) closed and Cromer (Beach) was used instead; after reversal there, some of the coaches went on to Sheringham.

Provision of the new Pacifics enabled the GE section to recast its main line timetables and regularise departure times, so from Monday 18th June 1951, *THE NORFOLKMAN* left Liverpool Street at 9.30 a.m. and Norwich at 5.45 p.m. The schedule was two hours and ten minutes to and from Norwich, and three hours to and from Cromer. With the Cromer station change, the restaurant car terminated there but some coaches went on to arrive in Sheringham at 1.06 p.m. They returned to Cromer at 4.20 p.m. from where the complete train left at 4.42 p.m. and from Norwich at 5.45 p.m. to reach London at 8.00 p.m. On Saturdays when three more coaches were included, an extra eleven minutes Down and ten Up were allowed. In the final Bradshaw (May 1961) the 9.30 a.m. reached Norwich at 11.43 a.m. where the

restaurant car was detached, and arrival at Cromer was 12.35 p.m., and Sheringham at 12.47 p.m. Returning at 4.35 p.m., from Cromer at 4.48 p.m. and Norwich at 5.45 p.m., there was 7.55 p.m. arrival at Liverpool Street and that applied also on Saturdays and by then diesel haulage had taken over.

For the first run Thompson B1 No.1236 had a headboard with white letters on a black painted plate in two lines. The plate was 12½ in. deep with incurved top corners but in 1950 it was replaced by a cast plate of the same size and shape, and that was the one used by the Pacifics.

WC/BB No.34059 worked the train during the 1949 trials and here at Norwich shed in May 1949, it awaits the evening return train to Liverpool Street. This particular appearance of a Southern Region Pacific on ex-GER lines was not to be the last.

In June 1949, Haymarket A4 No.60027 MERLIN, in dark blue livery, has *THE CAPITALS LIMITED* heading through Peterborough. This locomotive did twenty consecutive double trips on this non-stop working.

THE CAPITALS LIMITED

Post-war, the non-stop *FLYING SCOTSMAN* ran just for the 1948 summer season, but for 1949 there was a significant change. Operative from 23rd May, the non-stop was changed from the traditional 10 o'clock to a 9.30 a.m. departure from London and 9.45 a.m. from Edinburgh, and these trains were given the name of *THE CAPITALS LIMITED*. Its introduction allowed the *FLYING SCOTSMAN* to retain the long-established 10 o'clock departure time, and also make very useful calls at Grantham and Newcastle.

Although the pre-war 'non-stop' had got the journey time down to just seven hours, the 1949 train needed an eight-hour timing. The 473 ton load of thirteen coaches, which included a kitchen car, buffet car, and two open restaurant cars was partly responsible, although some of the extended time stemmed from the cautious traversing of the replacement bridges and track which had been washed away in August 1948 by the floods between Berwick and Dunbar.

By 1950 it was possible to cut the Down train time to seven hours and forty minutes, and that of the Up train to seven hours and forty-five minutes. For the 1951 summer, the load was limited to twelve coaches, and the time came down to seven hours twenty minutes in both directions. Then for 1952, the maximum was eleven coaches, enabling Edinburgh to be reached in just six minutes over seven hours, whilst southbound it was seven minutes over the same number of hours. A minor change for that year was to a 9.35 a.m. instead of the usual 9.30 a.m. departure from King's Cross. Normally regarded as a London-Edinburgh service

(given further emphasis by its name), it did also serve Dundee and Aberdeen for which through coaches were included both ways. By 1952 these had reduced the London to Aberdeen time to almost exactly eleven hours.

The non-stop running between the two capital cities necessitated the use of engines which had a corridor type tender enabling crews to be changed en route. All twenty-two tenders of that type were then coupled to the A4 class engines which limited the non-stop working to that class, and also to those engines shedded at King's Cross and at Haymarket. Anything else seen on that train indicated a failure somewhere along the line, such as Peppercorn A1 No.60151 being photographed on the Up train running 110 minutes late at Potters Bar on Saturday 21st July 1951. On the previous Wednesday, a failure at Alnmouth led to two D20's, Nos.62331 and 62383

taking the train on to Newcastle, whence Peppercorn A1 No.60121 took it on to King's Cross. In contrast to those blemishes, one should note that 60022 did twenty-three trips, whilst 60029 did thirty-seven and 60027 did twenty-six double trips, twenty of them consecutively.

From the May 1949 start, the engine headboard was of the cast type with beaded edge and raised, polished lettering. It had square top corners with the legend in two lines, THE CAPITALS above LIMITED. Named as such, that train's final runs were on Saturday 13th September 1952 because, when resumed for the 1953 summer, the name was changed to *THE ELIZABETHAN*.

A4 No.60011 was another Haymarket favourite for this job and here in 1949, still in LNER Garter blue, it has the Up train south of Chaloners Whin. Note that the headboard is in the lower lamp iron position.

(above) Before its name was changed in time for the 1953 season, the headboard of *THE CAPITALS LIMITED* gained the coat-of-arms of London and Edinburgh and whereas these 'marks' were usually placed on the upper portion of a headboard, in this case they sat either side of the last word. No.60024 was another Haymarket engine and has the Up train near Chaloners Whin.

(opposite) A King's Cross A4 this time, though in this August 1950 view their is no indication of its home shed. No.60008 was recently ex works although 'Top Shed' normally turned out its A4's with this kind of finish. This dramatic view at Naburn swing bridge emphasises the superb lines of the ultimate Gresley Pacific.

(right) Not to curry too much favour with the A4's on this working, here is a picture featuring a none too clean Peppercorn A1, No.60151 of Gateshead, heading a very late Up train near Potters Bar in July 1951.

A4's figured prominently on *THE ELIZABETHAN* and anything else was a stand-in for a failure. Here 60024 heads a Down Saturday working through Peterborough in September 1953. By now the coaching stock is becoming a little bit more standardised in both type and painting.

In the final year of regular steam haulage 60033 of King's Cross made just one return trip on this train though in the intervening years it clocked up dozens. Escrick.

(opposite) After its slow progress through York station, 60010 picks up the pace, passing Clifton locomotive shed, whilst in charge of the Down train in the 1950's.

THE ELIZABETHAN

In order to celebrate the Coronation of Queen Elizabeth II, BR renamed the *THE CAPITALS LIMITED* to *THE ELIZABETHAN*. The first runs of *THE ELIZABETHAN* were made on Monday 29th June 1953, and then resumed for each summer season, until at the end of the 1961 season on Friday 8th September, when the last steam hauled runs were made. Being non-stop between London and Edinburgh in both directions, only corridor tender fitted A4 class could be used, the sheds at King's Cross and Haymarket being those to provide them.

By 1961, BR's attitude regarded steam as outmoded and 'to be dispensed with as soon as possible'. That year, on *THE ELIZABETHAN*, the A4's showed how short-sighted a policy that was, and their performance also completely destroyed the detractors of the Gresley 2 to 1 derived valve gear. Twenty-five years old 60014 did no less than twenty return trips, six of them consecutively; only one failure occurred, No.60030 having to come off the 31st August Down trip at Newcastle due to injector trouble. (The train was taken on to Edinburgh by A3 No.60040). From King's Cross 60022 and 60029 were the others used, whilst 60033 just made one return trip. Haymarket's reputation for reliability was fully maintained; they only used three, 60009, 60024 and 60031. The final trips were done by distinguished engines, 60022 on the last Down and 60009 on the last Up train.

The inaugural time for the journey was $6^3/4$ hours but in 1954 that was reduce to $6^1/2$ hours or only 390 minutes start to stop for the 392.7 miles. From 1962, Deltics took over and whilst nominally non-stop to passengers, they halted briefly at Newcastle for crew changing.

The two cast headboards were the full $14^3/8$, in. depth with incurved top corners, the name being in two lines. The customary carrying position was on the centre lamp iron at buffer beam level but it was not unusual to see one on the upper lamp iron, trains in both directions being so observed.

60031 GOLDEN PLOVER was another Haymarket regular on the 'non-stop'. Here it has the Down train at Selby on an unknown date.

(above) Working hard between the tunnels at Belle Isle, 60027 MERLIN lifts the northbound train out of King's Cross in 1960.

(right) Having completed its task, running more than 392 miles non-stop with the last steam worked Up train on the 8th September 1961, 60009 rests at the buffer stops in King's Cross terminus. Happily, this locomotive, along with the engine that handled the last Down working, are now preserved.

THE WHITE ROSE

Starting on 23rd May 1949 a new morning service from London to Leeds and Bradford was named *THE WHITE ROSE*. From King's Cross at 9.18 a.m. it was non-stop to Doncaster and the Leeds arrival was at 1.00 p.m. On Tuesdays and Saturdays during the currency of the winter timetable, this train carried a portion with a restaurant car for Tyne Commission Quay, to serve the boat for Norway. That was detached at Doncaster and worked forward by NE Region.

Although aimed at businessmen desirous of visiting the two West Yorkshire cities, British Railway's typical dickering with its London departure times must have been both irritating and equally frustrating to them. Until the summer of 1953 it left at 9.18 a.m. then changed to 9.10 a.m., going back to 9.18 a.m. in the winter timetable. In the 1954 summer it had a ridiculous move to as early at 8.50 a.m. then the next timetable put it back again to 9.10 a.m. from King's Cross. In the May 1961 timetable it was leaving at 9.20 a.m. Could anything be likelier to drive busy men into deserting it in favour of using the M1 motorway?

The return train did not offer any greater attraction either. Originally it left Leeds at 5.15 p.m. and took four hours to reach King's Cross. That was soon altered to a 3.15 p.m. departure and 7.56 p.m. arrival, changed in the summer of 1953 to 3.20 p.m. and 7.40 p.m. respectively. The next timetable altered it again to 3.25 p.m. and 7.34 p.m. Even that slight improvement still drove users into waiting for *THE QUEEN OF SCOTS* Pullman, which gave another hour and ten minutes in Leeds and yet was only sixteen minutes later into King's Cross at 7.50 p.m. Steam was never given a fair chance to show what it could do with this named train because even in May 1961, with stops only at Wakefield and Doncaster it still took four hours with times of 3.32 p.m. and 7.32 p.m. At no time did it deserve named train status, and especially when rostered for Pacific duty.

King's Cross shed normally sent out an engine approaching the need for a general repair. Also it was no surprise to see A1/1 No.60113 working it prior to Top Shed getting rid of it in June 1950. A4's did work it as on 28th June 1958 when 60017 SILVER FOX had the Down train, but was then well over a year since its previous 'general'.

Two types of headboard were made for it, the first a flat plate painted black with white lettering and with square top corners. That was soon replaced by the standard cast type with incurved top corners, which was then carried to the end of steam haulage.

(opposite) Copley Hill A1 No.60114 takes the late afternoon departure of *THE WHITE ROSE* out of Leeds (Central) in 1950. The austere headboard of the period did nothing for the reputation of this train.

(right) Thompson A1/1 No.60113 heads the morning departure to Leeds through New Barnet in 1950. Notice that a BR standard cast headboard now adorns the smokebox. Two white rose emblems would eventually sit either side of THE to complete the style of *THE WHITE ROSE* headboard.

Peppercorn A1's were the preferred motive power for *THE WEST RIDING*. Within this, Down, train's consist were six of the original *WEST RIDING LIMITED* carriages suitably refurbished. Besides the more usual cast headboard, No.60123 has another board at footplate level displaying three reels of wool over the title of the train. Wymondley, 6th June 1952.

THE WEST RIDING

Monday 23rd May 1949 saw the start of this train, which had a real pedigree and well merited naming. Since far back into Great Northern years there had been a 7.50 a.m. breakfast car train from Leeds to King's Cross, with a corresponding return around 4 o'clock from London. Then in the LNER peak years of 1937-1939, the streamlined *WEST RIDING LIMITED* had cut the journey time to just under 2³/₄ hours.

The 1949 train inherited features from both of these predecessors. It continued the 7.50 a.m. Leeds departure and returned from London at 3.45 p.m. with journey times around 3³/₄ hours. From the luxurious streamlined train it gained a set of six refurbished coaches which had been built in 1937. These had been stored in Leeds Copley Hill (*see* page 173) carriage sheds during the war, but were now put to further good use.

This morning train to London called at Wakefield and Doncaster and then ran non-stop, but the return called only at Wakefield where, in both directions, good connections by local trains served Bradford. The timing remained substantially the same until 2nd November 1959, although by 1954, Bradford had been given through coaches attached and detached at Wakefield. The afternoon return

"West Riding" then lost its name because that was transferred to the 7.45 a.m. from King's Cross, which called at Hitchin, Retford and Doncaster before splitting at Wakefield to give a Leeds arrival at 11.38 a.m. and 11.56 a.m. at Bradford. The Up train timings became 7.00 a.m. from Bradford and 7.30 a.m. from Leeds, combining at Wakefield and calling only at Doncaster with an 11.15 a.m. arrival in King's Cross, that train retaining *THE WEST RIDING* title.

In the years 1949-1959 both trains were rostered to be worked by a Peppercorn A1 shedded at Leeds Copley Hill, and always loaded to thirteen or fourteen

coaches. Occasionally, substitutions had to be made and a King's Cross A4 No.60006 took the Down train one afternoon in the 1949 summer. Then, sometime in 1957, Copley Hill borrowed Thompson A2/3 No.60521 and used it on the Up train. That Leeds shed had just been transferred from Eastern the N.E. Region responsibility.

From the May 1949 start, the headboard was a cast plate with incurved top corners showing THE above WEST RIDING, which continued to be carried until the end of haulage by steam.

Thompson A2/3 No.60521 backs out of King's Cross terminus in 1957 after arrival with *THE WEST RIDING* from Leeds. This Gateshead Pacific probably got to Leeds with the *QUEEN OF SCOTS* and was then commandeered by Copley to work the Up train

(above, left) Thompson B1's from Stratford brought *THE FENMAN* from London to Cambridge. 61361 has the Down train at Burnt Hill on the 7th August 1950.

(above) Both Stratford and Cambridge B17's took their turn on this named train during the 1950's. 61643 has the Up train on the last day of August 1951.

(left) B2 No.61617 of Cambridge shed takes its turn on the London working and is at Littlebury in 1953.

THE FENMAN

This name was applied from 23rd May 1949 to a long-established service from Hunstanton to and from London which dated from Great Eastern days. In the July 1922 timetable a through train left Hunstanton at 7.02 a.m. called at King's Lynn, Ely, Cambridge and Bishop's Stortford and arrived in Liverpool Street at 10.23 a.m. It had a restaurant car for the full journey and at Cambridge 1st and 3rd class Pullman cars were added; they had started from Bury St Edmunds at 7.36 a.m. Return was at 4.45 p.m., the same calls were made and Hunstanton arrival was at 7.50 p.m. That train included the restaurant car but the Pullmans for Bury followed later and they ceased to run when the LNER took over at the beginning of 1923.

In the summer of 1938, the Hunstanton departure was at 7.12 a.m. with the same calls and a car serving breakfasts to arrive in London at 10.23 a.m. On Mondays only, the times were 7.41 a.m. and 10.30 a.m. From London there was still the 4.45 p.m. departure, the same calls, and Hunstanton was reached at 7.50 p.m. The effect of the 1939-1945 war on this train can be seen in the final LNER timetable which was current from 6th October 1947. To keep the 10.30 a.m. London arrival and include an extra call at Audley End, the Hunstanton departure had to be as early as 6.45 a.m. From London, the departure moved to 4.30 p.m. and it was into Hunstanton at 8.09 p.m. That had no call at Audley End, but did have a buffet car as far as Ely.

When named in May 1949, there was modest improvement in the running time, and the addition of a portion from, and back to, Bury St Edmunds via Cambridge. With the Hunstanton departure still at 6.45 a.m., that then gave a Liverpool Street arrival at 10.03 a.m.; Bury passengers had left at 7.57 a.m.. The 4.30 p.m. departure from London was retained and arrivals were 6.45 p.m. at Bury and 7.55 p.m. at Hunstanton.

The 1951 introduction of Pacifics on the Ipswich line had no effect on *THE FENMAN* and it was the 1953 summer when change took place. The train ceased to serve Bury (which gained its own trains to and from London) but a portion was included to serve March and Wisbech (East) via Ely. The Hunstanton departure became 6.50 a.m., that from Wisbech 7.30 a.m. and London arrival was advanced to 9.53 a.m. Return remained at 4.30 p.m., arriving Wisbech at 7.03 p.m. and Hunstanton at 7.35 p.m. and to which there was a restaurant car which had served breakfasts on the morning train.

By May 1961 *THE FENMAN* ran only from and to King's Lynn, Hunstanton having to make do with a connecting diesel railcar. Departure was at 7.46 a.m. and London arrival was at 9.56 a.m. with a call at Downham replacing that at Bishop's Stortford. The return at 4.36 p.m. reached King's Lynn at 6.53 p.m. and a restaurant/buffet car was included in both directions.

On the Cambridge-London section, the usual engine was a Cambridge shedded B17 (or a B2), or one of Stratford's B1 class, but north of Cambridge there could be interesting variety. Even into the 1950's, Great Eastern built engines were still being used, especially whilst the Bury portion was included. That often had an Ipswich based B12/3 or D16/3 and on one occasion J15 No.65447, which had been built in 1899, deputised for a failure and duly carried the headboard. That was one of the British Railways cast type with incurved corners at the top with *THE FENMAN* set in two lines and there was no variation of it.

J15 No.65447 was most unexpected motive power on the Bury portion. Cambridge, 13th September 1951.

A4 No.60003 leaves York for the south with the Up *NORTHUMBRIAN* in 1950. The headboard is the earliest version.

(opposite) A3's such as No.60062 were regular performers on *THE NORTHUMBRIAN*.

THE NORTHUMBRIAN & THE NORTH BRITON

The 1949 winter service, from 26th September, was the first to confer names onto two long established trains - a pair of Newcastle to London business expresses becoming *THE NORTHUMBRIAN*. These trains were the 10.00 a.m. from Newcastle and the 12.20 p.m. ex King's Cross. The other naming was a real break-through because of the first time a train for which the North Eastern was responsible was named and carried a headboard.

From 1910 to 1922 the North Eastern Railway did no naming and from 1923 to 1947 the North Eastern Area of the LNER firmly avoided that issue. Even the North Eastern Region of British Railways took almost two years to achieve that objective. As far back at 1901, the NER put on a through Leeds (New) to Edinburgh train and in 1910 it was extended to Glasgow. Leaving Leeds around 9 o'clock, Glasgow was reached just before 3.00 p.m.

and the 4.00 p.m. departure returned the set of coaches to Leeds at 10.00 p.m., a trip of 555 miles each day.

The restaurant cars on that train served all four meals of the day, breakfast, luncheon, tea and dinner and if ever a train earned the distinction of being named, this one did. From 26th September 1949 it became *THE NORTH BRITON* and carried a standard cast headboard.

A1 No.60157 of Grantham shed has *THE NORTHUMBRIAN* in 1955. By now the headboard has acquired embellishments featuring the arms of London and Northumberland.

(opposite) Battling a cold day in February 1953, A4 No.60028 has the train at Croft.

Copley Hill shed was responsible for the southern leg of *THE NORTH BRITON* and A1 No.60133 was photographed in 1950, fresh from repair, with the headboard.

(opposite) Between Edinburgh and Glasgow B1 haulage was not unusual. Here, Eastfield's No.61340, complete with headboard, gets *THE NORTH BRITON* off on the final leg of its outward journey in September 1954. The stock, and the catering staff aboard, would make the return leg to Leeds - a total distance of 555 miles - an hour after the Glasgow arrival.

THE TYNESIDER - THE EASTERLING - THE BROADSMAN

When the 1950 summer service became effective on 5th June, three more new names came in - all carried on standard board with top corners indented. The 10.35 p.m. Newcastle-King's Cross and the 11.45 p.m. King's Cross to Newcastle sleeping car trains were titled *THE TYNESIDER*.

Running only in the summer - in 1950 from 5th June to 23rd September - was *THE EASTERLING*, a joint service at 11.03 a.m. from Liverpool Street to Yarmouth (South Town) and to Lowestoft, with division at Beccles after a non-stop run from London. Both portions began their return at 7.10 p.m. joined at Beccles, and then ran non-stop for a 10.00 p.m. arrival in Liverpool Street. The third new name was

THE BROADSMAN, an all-year round service to give North Norfolk people a useful time in London. Starting from Sheringham at 6.03 a.m. and from Cromer at 6.28 a.m., and after its reversal, leaving Norwich at 7.30 a.m., Liverpool Street arrival was at 10.16 a.m. The return train left London at 3.40 p.m. giving arrivals at Norwich of 6.16 p.m., Cromer at 7.15 p.m. and Sheringham at 7.43 p.m. After running to these times for just a year, they were cut substantially in June 1951 and further still in September 1952, when the Down train got the first mile-a-minute run ever in East Anglia - Ipswich to Norwich 46.3 miles in 45 minutes.

Author's note: Due to the nocturnal nature of *THE TYNESIDER*, it has been impossible to secure photographic evidence of its habits.

(opposite) B1 No.61171 is not looking its best in this August 1951 view of *THE EASTERLING* approaching Chelmsford. The Stratford based Thompson engines were staple motive power for this summer only period train. Note the embellished headboard.

(below) In the summer of 1953, Stratford shed were still using B17's on *THE EASTERLING* and No.61668 not only has the latest headboard but is showing discs also.

THE BROADSMAN was an all-year round service and B1 No.61050 has been suitably cleaned by Norwich shed. Here, in November 1950 at Liverpool Street, the train is waiting for its afternoon departure.

Seen at Gunton, L1 No.67798 has the Sheringham and Cromer portions of the Down train, with a headboard in place, after its reversal and engine change at Norwich.

Haymarket shed were responsible for the London bound *HEART OF MIDLOTHIAN* and their A2/1 No.60507 speeds south near Burnmouth on the 12th April 1952. Note the headboard is in the lower position.

(left) Gateshead shed also had a hand with this train and A1 No.60124 has a Down train on the ECML in 1954.

(opposite) Gateshead A1, No.60150 has the Down *THE HEART OF MIDLOTHIAN* nicely wound up on the ECML racetrack between Beningbrough and Tollerton.

THE HEART OF MIDLOTHIAN

1951 was Festival of Britain year and the South Bank Exhibition on the Thames was expected to generate appreciable extra traffic to London. To mark their connection with it, British Railways specially named five main-line expresses for the start of the 1951 summer service on 18th June. These trains were also equipped with new BR standard coaches and restaurant cars.

On what had been the LNER, the service selected for naming and new stock was the afternoon counterparts of *THE FLYING SCOTSMAN*. These had been running since well before the 1914 war with both London and Edinburgh starting times varying between 1.00 p.m. and 2.20 p.m. From 7th May 1951, these became 2.00 p.m. from King's Cross and from Waverley and they were named *THE HEART OF MIDLOTHIAN*. As a temporary measure, one at least carried a painted plate with white lettering on A black background but both were soon equipped with a standard cast headboard. The southbound train (only) had through coaches from Aberdeen attached to it in Waverley and both trains continued their established all-year operation.

This A4 presents a classic pose heading *THE TALISMAN* through Harringay and out of London in 1961.

THE TALISMAN - THE FAIR MAID

Three years passed before any further trains were named and again it was on a London-Edinburgh service. On 17th September 1956 *THE TALISMAN* began operation, giving a 4.00 p.m. departure both from King's Cross and Waverley. The time of six hours forty minutes included a six minute stop at Newcastle, convenient alike for passengers and engine change. This permitted the use of Class A3 and A4 engines which did not have a corridor tender. The train was a Monday to Friday service and a link with the pre-war *CORONATION* 4.00 p.m. departures was that each set of stock included the twin first class coaches from those trains. The other nine coaches in each were new ones to BR standards.

From the start of the 1957 summer service on 17th June, two more trains titled *THE TALISMAN* began to run. The 7.45 a.m. from King's Cross arrived Edinburgh at 2.30 p.m. enabling the coaches to be used for the 4.00 p.m. return train. Similarly a 7.30 a.m. departure from Waverley provided the coaches for the 4.00 p.m. from King's Cross. All four trains carried *THE TALISMAN* headboard.

From 16th September 1957, to obviate confusion, the morning trains were re-named *THE FAIR MAID* as they were extended to and from Perth, via the Forth Bridge; they also had the by now standard headboard. Departures were altered to 7.50 a.m. from London and 8.30 a.m. from Edinburgh but this Perth extension made it impossible for the coaches to take up the afternoon return workings. *THE FAIR MAID* only ran to the end of the 1958 summer workings, that is for just a year, as the Edinburgh-Perth extension was then dropped, and the two morning trains again became *THE TALISMAN*. They did however retain the 7.50 a.m. London and 8.30 a.m. Edinburgh departures.

On the morning of 13th July 1959 dirty A1 No.60159 has charge *THE TALISMAN* at Newcastle.

Drifting through Darlington with the renamed morning version of *THE TALISMAN*, A1 No.60156 has *THE FAIR MAID*.

King's Cross A4 No.60015 has *THE FAIR MAID* at York in summer 1958, the last season in which the morning trains ran with that name. A4's figure prominently in this tome but, considering they were small in number compared to other classes, they also figured prominently on the ECML.

Both A3's and A4 with non-corridor tenders were able to be used on *THE TALISMAN*. Here A3 No.60039 exits Gasworks tunnel with the Down train.

BR Standard No.70000 BRITANNIA at Clacton in June 1958 has *THE ESSEX COAST EXPRESS* for the first Up service. This specially made headboard was apparently used just the once.

THE ESSEX COAST EXPRESS

During 1958, new English Electric 2000 h.p. diesel electric locomotives took over the London - Norwich expresses and this released some BR Standard Pacific engines for an improved commuter service between Clacton and Liverpool Street. One of these, the 7.51 a.m. from Clacton and the return from London at 5.27 p.m. was named *THE ESSEX COAST EXPRESS*.

In line with promotional efforts, the inaugural Up run, on 9th June 1958, was hauled by No.70000 BRITANNIA carrying a circular headboard of about the same diameter as the smokebox door. In normal service, a standard headboard was used. No evidence has been found that any ex-LNER locomotive (B1, B12/3, B17 or anything else) ever hauled this train, the only train dealt with in this monograph not to have had that honour. This particular train headboard could have been a Stratford production as its lettering is somewhat smaller than that used on the headboards made at Doncaster.

BR 'Britannia' No.70003 carries the more conventional headboard. Note the overhead electrical catenary which would soon bring about another motive power change on these Clacton trains.

V2 No.60846 of Thornaby shed has the new Up train named *THE TEES-THAMES* with the temporary headboard in 1960.

(opposite) No.60103 again has *THE TEES-THAMES* and is ready for the afternoon departure from King's Cross. Note that the headboard is in a different position this time.

(below) FLYING SCOTSMAN passes Peterborough with *THE TEES-THAMES* on its afternoon return to the North East. By now the headboard is of the standard type. Note the 'shape of things to come' on the left.

THE TEES-THAMES

Despite the increasing use of diesel locomotives, a new steam-hauled named train began to run on Monday 2nd November 1959 when the winter service started. This was *THE TEES-THAMES* which left Saltburn at 7.05 a.m., served Middlesbrough,

and arrived at King's Cross at 12.15 p.m.

The return departure was at 2.00 p.m., terminating in Saltburn at 7.23 p.m. At first, a temporary plate headboard was used with a white painted name on a black background. As this was

done in a single line it was cramped, even with smaller lettering than usual. Quite quickly, however, a standard cast headboard was provided.

ANGLO-SCOTTISH CAR CARRIER

The final regular train to which a name, and a cast headboard was applied began on 30th May 1960 as the *ANGLO-SCOTTISH CAR CARRIER*. The headboard as one of the few with square top corners and without THE to its name.

This train left Holloway car loading bay (just north of King's Cross station) at 7.50 a.m. daily (except Sundays) in the summer service, with arrivals at Newcastle (Central) at 12.30 p.m. and in Edinburgh (Waverley) at 2.45 p.m. Southbound, it left Edinburgh at 11.40 a.m., Newcastle at 1.55 p.m. to reach Holloway at 6.30 p.m. There were also some overnight similar trains known as *CAR SLEEPER LIMITED* but only the day trains of 1960 onward carried any headboard, and only when steam hauled.

A dirty A4, No.60025, has charge of the Up *ANGLO-SCOTTISH CAR CARRIER* at Welwyn tunnels in June 1963.

(below) One of the car carrying vehicles used for the *ANGLO-SCOTTISH CAR CARRIER*.

DECORATIONS ON HEADBOARDS

Embellishment of headboards was entirely a British Railways innovation, first seen at the beginning of June 1950 when coloured plaques of the Dutch and British Flags were affixed in the top corners of *THE DAY CONTINENTAL* headboard. On the black background these did not show to advantage, and they were soon replaced by circular plaques with a white background on which the flags were more easily seen. They were still being displayed in this form during May 1956. The headboard of *THE HOOK CONTINENTAL* was treated exactly the same, originally just the Flags and then circular plaques with white background. *THE SCANDINAVIAN* of course had Danish and British Flags and as it was appreciably later than the other two in getting the standard cast headboard, it got circular plaques from the start.

Others on the G.E. line to get decorated headboards were:-

THE BROADSMAN - a yacht and windmill on one side, and a Norfolk wherry and a windmill on the other. This was the only one noted on which the plaque positions were reversed.

THE EASTERLING - the arms of Yarmouth and of Lowestoft.

THE EAST ANGLIAN - the arms of London and of Norwich.

No evidence has been found that any additions were made to the headboards of *THE NORFOLKMAN*, *THE FENMAN* and *THE ESSEX COAST EXPRESS*.

On the GN line there was a similar broad division between those which had and those which had not. Headboards not embellished were *THE TALISMAN, THE QUEEN OF SCOTS, THE HEART OF MIDLOTHIAN, THE TEES-THAMES, TYNE-TEES PULLMAN, THE NIGHT SCOTSMAN, THE WEST RIDONG, THE YORKSHIRE PULLMAN, THE ELIZABETHAN, THE FAIR MAID* and *ANGLO-SCOTTISH CAR CARRIER*. Against these eleven there were nine which did get headboard additions. They were first seen on 6th June 1950, and the following got them:-

THE FLYING SCOTSMAN - rose and thistle intertwined.

THE ABERDONIAN - arms of London and of Aberdeen.

THE SCARBOROUGH FLYER - segment of sun with rays from them.

THE CAPITALS LIMITED - arms of London and of Edinburgh.

THE WHITE ROSE - two Yorkshire tudor roses.

THE TYNESIDER - arms of London and of Newcastle.

THE NORTHUMBRIAN - arms of London and of Northumberland.

THE HARROGATE SUNDAY PULLMAN - arms of London and of Harrogate.

THE NORSEMAN - two Viking ships.

On the GC Line, *THE SOUTH YORKSHIREMAN* got no addition, nor did the stainless steel plate on *THE MASTER CUTLER*, but a standard cast headboard for the latter had the arms of London and of Sheffield added.

The NE Region made no addition to *THE NORTH BRITON* nor did Scottish Region to *THE FIFE COAST EXPRESS*.

These additional discs and shield shaped badges tended to come off in service and from the mid-1950's, it was possible to see headboards carrying only one of the pair even on such a prestigious train as *THE FLYING SCOTSMAN*. By 1960 such headboards as were still being used were normally devoid of embellishments. For two weeks at the time of Queen Elizabeth's Coronation in June 1953, the engines working *THE FLYING SCOTSMAN* and *THE WEST RIDING* carried the usual headboard and also a gaily painted appropriate plate. Finally, in March/April 1962, what had been *THE WHITE ROSE* carried a large circular headboard (*see* page 302) as B.R. support for a wool promotion campaign.

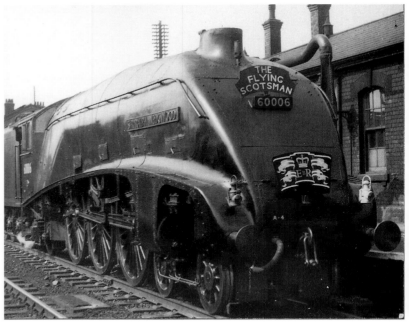

The additional appropriate headboard caried on *THE FLYING SCOTSMAN* during the two week Coronation period of June 1953.

The March/April 1962 alternative WHITE ROSE headboard promoting the Yorkshire wool campaign and as worn by A3 No.60107 on the Up train at Doncaster on the 12th April.

A selection of BR headboards hang on the rack at King's Cross in 1961. A couple are *sans* embellishments.

BR PERIOD HOLIDAY TRAINS

BUTLIN EXPRESS

BUTLIN'S EXPRESS

SHEFFIELD SEASIDE EXPRESS

C.T.A.C. SCOTTISH TOURS EXPRESS

HOLIDAY CAMPS EXPRESS

BUTLIN EXPRESS & HOLIDAY CAMP EXPRESSES

Throughout the 1950's the big Butlin Holiday Camps at Skegness and Clacton generated enough summer Saturday traffic to warrant running special trains for them, from King's Cross to Skegness and from Liverpool Street to Clacton. Headboards were carried on both, but were treated differently. The GE Line used a circular board of similar diameter to the smokebox with *BUTLIN EXPRESS* on it, but the GN Line provided a plate of standard shape, with scalloped top corners painted white with *BUTLIN'S EXPRESS* in black.

These holiday specials had a long history and carried headboards both before and after the LNER years. From Nottingham in 1922 one was running with a GNR destination board specially extended to three lines showing Skegness, Sutton-on-Sea and Mablethorpe. Some thirty-six years later, in August 1958, Sheffield provided a standard shape plate with a black background and lettered in white *SHEFFIELD SEASIDE EXPRESS*, for one of their trains to Bridlington.

Trains to the seaside were not the only ones to carry a headboard. In the 1950's a series of them ran sufficiently often for a cast headboard to be made. Of standard shape with indented top corners, it carried *C.T.A.C. SCOTTISH TOURS EXPRESS*. The initials stand for Creative Tourist Agents' Conference who,

in the summer months, from 1950 to 1962, ran a series of all-inclusive tours to Scotland. These did not appear in the public timetable but the working timetables show them as starting from the Manchester Area and also from Sheffield originally, but later from Chesterfield, Nottingham and Leicester. In 1956 the train left Leicester at 5.20 a.m. and ran through to Craigendoran.

After the 1939-1945 war there was tremendous growth in holiday camps and on the fifteen miles of coast from Lowestoft northwards they were almost continuous. Apart from the named trains to Butlin camps, there was a series of trains in the summer timetables which were designated *HOLIDAY CAMPS EXPRESS* and taking 1953 as an example, there were as many as eight from and to Liverpool Street. Most of these had a buffet car included but none of them carried an engine headboard.

They ran on Saturdays only, with the London departures spread between 7.58 a.m. and 3.00 p.m. First away, at 7.58 a.m., was one which called only at Ipswich and Beccles to arrive in Lowestoft at 10.45 a.m., where it reversed and then served Corton, Hopton-on-sea and Gorleston where it terminated at 11.17 a.m. Next was a 10.15 a.m. departure, making the same stops and reaching Gorleston at 1.37 p.m. Another at 11.12 a.m. took the same route but called at seven more stations between Ipswich and Lowestoft so that it was 2.58 p.m. when it got to Gorleston. They were completed by a 3.00 p.m. which ran non-stop from Liverpool Street to Lowestoft for a 5.33 p.m. arrival, and then Corton and Hopton calls to finish at 6.30 p.m.

In the other direction a 10.45 a.m. from Gorleston called at Hopton and at Corton but halted

outside Lowestoft to reverse and change engines and then ran non-stop to Liverpool Street at 1.53 p.m. Next was a 1.35 p.m. from Gorleston, which made Corton, Hopton, Lowestoft, Oulton Broad, Beccles and Ipswich calls to reach London at 5.01 p.m., so only two Up workings contrasted with four Down trains.

At Gorleston these trains were 2½ miles south of Yarmouth and another pair of *HOLIDAY CAMP EXPRESSES* served Caister-on-Sea, just 2¾ miles north of Yarmouth, but they took a totally different route. From Liverpool Street at 10.50 a.m. the Down train took the Cambridge and Ely line to the avoiding curve at Norwich on to the Cromer line to make its first advertised stop at Wroxham at 2.10 p.m.

It then ran through North Walsham on to the Mundesley branch where it reversed at Antingham Road Junction on to the former M. &G.N. line to call at Potter Heigham, Hemsby and Caister Camp Halt, finishing with a 3.22 p.m. arrival at Caister-on-Sea. The Up train left Caister-on-Sea at 10.41 a.m., made the same calls, took the same route and was in to London at 3.27 p.m.

(opposite) B1 No.61139 has the GN Line version of the *BUTLIN'S EXPRESS* headboard in June 1958 en route from King's Cross to Skegness. As usual, 'Top Shed' has turned out one of its locomotives in the accepted manner for a special working.

This rather technically undesirable image has been included to show the GE Line version of the *BUTLIN EXPRESS* headboard as worn by B17 No.61651.

(left) B1 No.61399 has one of the holiday camp expresses in tow in the late 1950's. Note the wording on the headboard - yet another variation on the theme.

(opposite) The *SHEFFIELD SEASIDE EXPRESS* headboard was probably locally made and had painted letters on a black background. Here on 7th August 1958, nicely turned-out B1 No.61153 of Darnall shed awaits its return working at Bridlington shed. Note the reporting number.

A3 No.2508 BROWN JACK of Haymarket shed drifts through Galashiels with a London (St Pancras) bound pre-war *THAMES-FORTH* express.

(opposite) A3 No.2745 CAPTAIN CUTTLE on the Waverley route with the Down *THAMES-FORTH* in 1929.

LNER PACIFICS ON LMS SCOTTISH NAMED TRAINS

The former Midland Railway, at great expense, built its Settle to Carlisle line so that it could participate in the lucrative traffic between London and Scotland. In the 1930's, its successor the LMS was running named trains to both Glasgow and Edinburgh, but with the Glasgow train - *THE THAMES-CLYDE* - the LNER had no connection. Not so with *THE THAMES-FORTH* to and from Edinburgh because they were responsible for its haulage over the 99 miles between Carlisle and Edinburgh. These trains were named in 1927, and the LNER responded to their increased prestige by allocating three new super-Pacifics (as they were then called) Class A3 Nos.2745, 2748 and 2749 to Carlisle Canal shed to work them. The LMS coaches carried the train name but no headboard was used although to and from Carlisle the LNER Pacific often carried a destination plate with St. Pancras or Edinburgh on it.

On 1st October 1945 both these trains were restored (and with restaurant cars included) and by 1950 the Glasgow train acquired a standard cast headboard, showing *THE THAMES-CLYDE EXPRESS*, but the Edinburgh train remained anonymous until 17th June 1957 when the 9.15 a.m. from St. Pancras and the 10.5 a.m. from Edinburgh were named *THE WAVERLEY* and the A3 class engines were provided with a standard cast headboard.

The introduction of main line diesel locomotives led to Class A3 Pacifics taking over in May 1960 of *THE THAMES-CLYDE EXPRESS* though from Leeds to Glasgow (St. Enoch), and back, and a headboard was carried but even by 2nd September 1961 the blight had set in, and the Down Glasgow train had a type 4 diesel carrying only 1S68 to identify it.

Meanwhile, ex LNER Pacifics of both classes A3 and A4 had been migrating steadily to Scottish Region sheds, and by the summer of 1962 were masters of the three-hour expresses between Glasgow (Buchanan St) and Aberdeen by the former Caledonian main line, a faster regular service than ever before achieved. The four main trains were still named; they *were THE GRAMPIAN, THE SAINT MUNGO, THE BON-ACCORD* and *THE GRANITE CITY*. From 1950 they had certainly carried standard cast headboards showing each of these four names, but only one case has been found of any of these headboards being carried by an ex-LNER locomotives working these trains. However, those Scottish trains do not come into the remit of this tome as they did not travel specifically on LNER Lines.

Headboards were occasionally required to be returned to the shed responsible for them by a locomotive hauling a train without a name. A loose headboard carrie
in the cab would have been an encumbrance and very prone to damage, and so they were usually carried in the reversed position on either bottom, or top, lamp iror
Here King's Cross A3 No.60055 heads out of Leeds, over the former LNWR route at Copley Hill, with a London bound express in 1960.